Adrenaline

Excitement

And

Fear

Jack Holder

Farabee Publishing
Arizona

To Steve
Jack Holder

Copyright © 2014 by Jack Holder

This book is a work of the memories of Jack Holder, WWII Veteran. All rights reserved. This book, or parts thereof, may not be reproduced in any form without permission. Written by Elizabeth Sawyer and edited by Farabee Publishing. Special acknowledgement to Charles Gabrean.

Farabee Publishing

P O Box 322

Chandler, AZ 85244

Library of Congress Control Number: 2014960193
ISBN: 978-163173022-1

Printed in the United States of America

Book Cover designed by: Akivda M

To Ruth Calabro,

my sweetheart and the love of my life

who encouraged me to write this book.

The heat of battle can best be described in three words: Adrenaline, excitement and fear. Make no mistake about it, there is always a brief moment of fear. But there is a vast difference between the moment of fear and being afraid. Being afraid is long lasting and promotes bad decisions. But when the Adrenaline starts to flow the moment of fear changes to…Excitement.

Jack Holder

Prologue	ix
Acknowledgements	xi
Boy From Texas	12
Farming in Newcastle	13
Grammar School and High School	16
Amusements in Newcastle	17
German Gas	28
Aviation	31
Joining Up	35
Pearl Harbor/Assignment in Paradise	48
Pearl Harbor Prior To 12/7/1941	54
Observation of Destruction	57
A Day That Will Live In Infamy	59
Aftermath	72
Leadership In The Pacific	75
Midway The War's Pivotal Battle	80
Guadalcanal/ Admiral Bull Halsey	91
European Theatre	104
Dunkeswell Devonshire, England	104
Post-WWII	114
Texco Oil Company	125
Allied Signal and Retirement	126
Navajo Code Talkers	127
Grand Marshal For Veterans Day Parade	129
Pearl Harbor: 73rd Anniversary	130
Publishers Remarks	139

Prologue

"Childhood grooms the man as time decides his future"

Hunkered down behind a fortress of sandbags on December 7, 1941, I wondered if this was the day I would die. That morning I watched as Japanese dive bombers devastated Pearl Harbor. I knew that we would no longer sit on the sidelines of the war ravaging Europe.

Hurriedly we prepared for another attack. We build makeshift machine gun pits around the perimeter of Ford Island. Watching, waiting, sleeping, our vigil lasted 72 hours. Those three nights delivered monotony and terror simultaneously. My two shipmates, Scribner and O'Leary, became my companions in the machine gun pit. We endured 72 hours of agonizing watch behind the walls of burlap and sand. Aimlessly, we took turns pointing the salvaged 50 caliber machine gun at the sky. I awoke that notorious Sunday a simple Texas farm boy. By nightfall my innocence stripped away, I had become a man.

My entry into the Navy resulted from my unwavering desire to escape the arduous Texas farm life of my parents.

Acknowledgements

I would like to thank the Chives Charities, and Timothy Davis of The Greatest Generation Organization, for the trip back to Pearl Harbor and Art Sloane, "Veterans Voice" Arizona Republic for encouraging me to tell my story.

Boy From Texas

I was born on December 13, 1921, in Gunter, Texas, located 15 miles outside of Dallas.

My Dad named me after his eldest brother, Joseph Norman Holder.

We moved from Gunter to the Profit Community, when I was one year old.

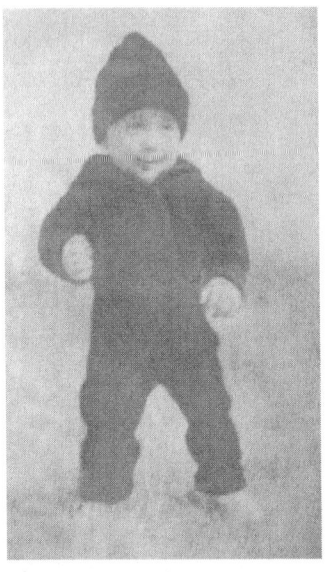

Jack at one year old

My Dad was only 2 when my Grandpa Holder died. Left with 5 small children Grandma re-married Grandpa Hudson who had 5 children of his own.

We moved into Grandma Hudson's home in the Profit Community while my Dad built a small 4 room framed house on the other side of Elm Creek.

My Dad was a farmer and WWI veteran. For those of you that are unfamiliar with farming it is a very primitive life.

We had no running water, no electricity, no phone, no bathroom and an outhouse in which we used the Sears and Roebuck catalogue for toilet paper. Our light came from kerosene lamps. Our cook stove burned wood for energy. Another wood burning stove heated the house. The closest telephone was a mile and a half away.

Farming in Newcastle

My parents were farmers, and the children of farmers. They knew nothing else.

Margaret and John E. Holder, Profit, Texas, 1935

Despite living through the depression, my parents fed us by producing the food they put on our table. But the three of us worked hard to get it there. Days started before the crack of dawn milking cows. We also picked and chopped cotton. Then I walked to school, came home to more farm chores, feeding chickens and hogs, I did homework by kerosene lamp.

Mother woke up before the rest of us long before dawn. Clad in a long dress and apron, she started preparing breakfast; bacon or ham, and scrambled eggs. My Mother had to have her coffee. Each morning she drank several cups of hot, black coffee. As Dad and I ate, she started preparing the cornbread and buttermilk and red beans for the dinner meal.

In the summer, Mother changed into her overalls so she could head out to the field after Dad and I finished breakfast.

Our 360 acre farm consisted of half pasture and half cultivation. We grew cotton, corn, wheat and oats. In addition we had a sizeable garden for Irish potatoes, green beans, okra, tomatoes, onions, squash, cantaloupe, watermelon and sweet potatoes.

Worker Hand Picking Cotton, September 21, 1936. Creator/Contributor: Claude C. ""Pop"" Laval, Fresno County Public Library

Out in the field we prepared the crops for picking cotton and maize. We used two different configurations to pick cotton. First, "pulling bowls" entailed pulling the entire pod from the cotton stalk. For the second method of picking cotton, I removed the cotton and seed from the pod while it remained on the stalk. My six-foot long canvas bag draped over my shoulder and dragged on the ground beside me. As I separated the ball, I plunged my roughened hands into the 2 foot opening and shoved in the cotton ball. When I filled the bag, I took it to the scales, weighed it, dumped out the cotton and then filled it all over again.

The maize grew about 6 feet high and produced a round bundle of seeds about 8 inches long. I cut the maize head from the stalk with a sharp knife then threw it into the wagon beside me. My sweat coupled with the plants dust created a terrible itch.

When darkness came, I headed to the barn to feed the hogs and chickens then milk the cows. Squeezing the cows' tits could be hazardous when their cocklebur infested tails slapped across my face. As tired as I would be I tried remaining alert enough to avoid facial lacerations.

Our family raised and butchered hogs and cattle. Dad smoked and cured the meat in the smoke house. We preserved the pork or beef by rubbing it with salt Dad also had a milk separator in the smoke house. This device separates the butter fat from the pure milk. My parents sold milk and butter from our dairy cows and traded at Phillips Grocery Store in Newcastle.

Grammar School and High School

I began school at 6 years old. A lot of the kids rode horses to school. I walked the mile to school every day. On my first day, I turned back and asked my Mother if I could have another pickle for my lunch. 1934 at 13 years of age I was a member of the Profit Community track team. I ran the 100 yard dash and chinned the bar. I chinned the bar 20 times and tied with another participant. We had to wait 2 hours and perform again. This time I went 22 times and placed first. I also won the 100 yard dash.

1935 I ran the 100 yard dash and placed first in chinned the bar.

1936 I won the 100 yard dash and placed second in chinned the bar. I went 60 times but my opponent went 66 times.

I played softball, volleyball, and captain of the basketball team for two years.

We played basketball on a dirt court.

When I began high school our transportation to Newcastle High School was a green Model A Ford truck driven by Jack Gates, with bench seats and canvas curtains. On cold days we practically froze as the canvas curtains flapped in the wind.

The football coach encouraged me to go out for the team. He wanted me to play halfback or running back. But, by the time the season started a new coach had arrived and he decided to put me on the line as a Guard. At 120 pounds I decided not to risk life and limb for the football team and I became a track star, captain of the basketball team and a softball player.

My talent in track and field landed me in the Pentathlon. As a Pent-athlete I ran the 100 yard dash, 220 yard low hurdle, 440 yard dash and the shot putt. My first year, I won first place in the county. The next year, I took first place in six county meets. The third year I won the Texas State Championship. I ran the 100 yard dash in 10 seconds flat and still today that is a commendable number.

Amusements in Newcastle

Aubrey McCarty, Charlie Terry, and I started our friendship when we began school. We would travel that mile together every school day to the Profit Community grammar school

We had one paved street; the one lane roadway ran between the Profit Community and Newcastle. Wet weather regularly rendered the more plentiful dirt roads impassable.

My Dad only traveled in our family Model T during pristine weather.

My Dad had a 1924 Model T Ford that was a bear to start. It required a hand crank and plenty of time to warm up. Dad's Model T ran on gasoline. Although it only cost 15 cents a gallon, gas presented other challenges. Every time he drove it, my thin but solid Dad jacked up the rear wheel, return to the front end and twist the crank. He insisted that jacking it up streamlined the starting process. I was skeptical.

Later on my Dad purchased a green 1928, 4 cylinder Chevrolet costing approximately $250. At 14, I learned to drive in this car.

1924-Ford-Model-T

Prone to broken drive shafts or rear axles, my Mother frequently sheared the Chevy's axle while on the 8 mile trip to buy fruit in Fort Belknap. The numerous breakdowns frustrated my Dad and in 1936 he bought a 1934 Chevrolet.

1934 Chevrolet Coup

My Mother washed and ironed, milked cows, fed chickens, worked in the field and managed to keep a pristine house. She was a tough cookie but had her fears and phobias.

I remember Mother would ring her hands in despair as she gazed out the kitchen window at threatening clouds gathering in the sky. Her fear was deep. With alarm, she turned to me. *"Jack, tell your Dad we need to get to the cellar"*.

Reluctantly, I got up from my homework and walked to the barn. There was no use arguing with my Mother when she spied any indication of a storm. But I knew my father's reaction before I arrived.

"Gosh Jack", my Dad exclaimed, *"that Mother of yours wants to board up the house if she feels a drop of rain! I don't think it is necessary to go to the cellar."* Dad turned back toward the smoke house and out of view.

My Dad was right. Mother feared storms and snakes.

I trudged back to the house. I leaned into the whipping wind pushing forward as if in slow motion. Mother had the cellar door open and waved me inside. She ushered me down into that large hole in the ground with a concrete top, floor and walls. The ceiling had two ventilators.

Mother smoothed her dress and secured her loose hair back into a bun. The ferocious whistle of the wind banged and battered the cellar door.

This time, Dad had miscalculated the seriousness of the storm. As the storm escalated, we could hear him hammering frantically on the door. Mother looked at the locked door and did not move.

His voice sounded faint and desperate as he cried *"Maggie, let me in."*

Mother folded her arms. A satisfied look spread across her face. *"Jack said you had work to do."*

"Maggie, please," he pleaded. Relenting my Mom let him in the cellar. He never teased her about her storm phobia again and she took every opportunity to remind him of the incident.

My Mother was a kind Christian woman, but had a very limited sense of humor. I once tested her patience by running a rope down the ventilator of our cellar as Mother stored peaches. I pushed the rope down one of the ventilators. Viewing her with one eye I aimed the rope to slide down the back of her dress.

The grin spread across my face as Mother wiggled uncomfortably then screeched and desperately grasped at her back trying to wrench the "snake" out of her dress. Howling she bounded up the rickety plank steps. She ran into the desert heat yanking the rope from inside her dress. I greeted her with hysterical laughter. My Mother failed to see the humor and quelled my laughter with a willow switch.

Mother was not afraid to discipline and had warned me not to get a whipping in school as I would return home to a worse one. I still recall the sting of a willow tree limb cracking against my bare legs.

Despite her strict nature and religious adherence, my Mother had a heart of gold and I was the focal point of her pride and nurturing. Despite all her responsibilities of keeping the house and laboring on the farm, my Mother washed our clothes thoroughly. *"You may go to school with patched clothes, Jack, but they will be clean."* She boiled the clothes in a large cast iron pot heated over a stack of the wood, I chopped while doing chores. Then she scrubbed the clothes on the wash board in the large galvanized wash tub which sat outside of the house.

Frank Heard, the Sheriff from the town of Thockmorton, neighbored us to the West and my friend Charlie Terry's family lived to the East. Charlie was as short and stout as I was lanky and skinny. We surveyed the neighborhood for mischief in the limited time we had between school, chores and homework.

Frank Heard adored his property and attended to it fanatically. One spring afternoon, Charlie and I stalked Frank as he vigorously dug deep holes along the perimeter of his property. Frank meticulously placed the pecans into the holes then covered them with inches of mulch. Ten times Frank repeated this process. Frank wiped the sweat from his brow, gathered the shovel and planting equipment and retreated toward the barn.

As darkness fell, Charlie and I emerged from our hiding spot and descended upon the freshly planted trees. Ten times we unearthed the newly planted pecans and gobbled up the delicious sweet-fleshed nuts.

In the following weeks, I saw Frank soaking his seeds. Frank frequented the ten spots to review the trees' progress.

"How those trees coming, Frank?" my Dad hollered from our yard.

"They aren't." Frank shook his head in disbelief. "*Texas must be too dry. Guess I'll need to head to Georgia or Alabama if I want pecan trees!*"

"Could be varmints." My Dad replied. He had no idea how right he was.

At 14 I gave home brewing a try. In secret, my friend, Charlie and I procured a wooden coke barrel and brought it to the large, hay-filled barn to begin our brewing. During the stifling heat of summer, the scent of fermenting spread throughout the barn. My father, on to our secret, tried to rile me saying *"Son, I believe someone must be making some home brew. You can smell it from a great distance."* When we finally opened our bottle of brew, it bubbled like champagne and was very ripe. That was our only attempt at home brewing.

My Mother faithfully opposed alcohol. Whenever I came home as a teenager she wanted to insure I had not been drinking but she couldn't smell and would instruct my Dad to smell my breath. He never did. He wasn't much of a drinker but I gave him a bottle of bourbon and he kept it in the bottom of a trunk hidden from my Mother. Years later he had that same bottle of bourbon in the trunk and every so often he would take a nip from it.

My maternal Grandmother equally disliked alcohol. After she lost two husbands, Grandmother moved in with my Uncle Arnold. Uncle Arnold was a confirmed bachelor at this point and used to doing as he pleased. One day, Grandmother discovered his stash of home brew. In order to impress upon him the evils of alcohol, she filled the jug with salt Later on, Uncle Arnold came home and wanted a drink. He filled a kitchen cup and took a sip. He reacted to the overpowering saltiness by spitting out the brew and smashing the cup. Grandmother told me that Arnold broke every cup in the kitchen trying to drink that brew. That spirited woman lived for 99 years and 11 months. She had a sound mind until the end and would fix her hair every morning before breakfast.

My paternal Grandmother lived with us for a spell. She doted on me, even splurging for the Charles Atlas fitness series for Christmas, a true luxury at the time. The previous Christmas my parents gave me an orange, banana and apple in the cane bottom chair in my room. I thought Grandmother a wonderful addition to the household.

I stood in the school playground shooting hoops and from a distance, I could see my father's 1934 Chevy kicking up dust as it hauled a large crate in the trunk. I couldn't wait to get home knowing the crate must contain the Sears and Roebuck radio from the catalogue. My anticipation mounting as I thought about listening to Amos and Andy.

"A 60th Anniversary Perspective on ... the Amos 'n' Andy TV Show" by EurWeb.com

My introduction to movies came when I walked into a canvas tent in rural Texas to see Charlie Chaplin's Silent City Lights. The noisy projector transported us from a weathered temporary tent to the busy city streets inhabited by the Tramp and his blind love interest. Sitting with my 10 cent ice cream, I thought nothing could be grander.

Charlie Chaplin's City Lights Poster

But my favorite diversion from the farm was the traveling medicine show. Aubrey, Charlie Terry and I never missed these performances. We would gather in town to enjoy the music, comedy, juggling, flea circuses, and magic tricks that accompanied the mesmerizing sales pitches. Fellows would turn their flatbed truck into a stage and present testimonials about the "miracle pills" or snake oil or ointment they were pitching. Some remedies proclaimed cures for tuberculosis, venereal disease, cancer, smoothing wrinkles, stain removal, even digestive problems. Elaborate stunts illustrated the healing powers of the performers' wares. Now and then an outfit even brought along sword and fire eating performers and even more unusual freaks.

Medicine Show

My life-long love of golf began at 14. I played my first round when a friend invited me to his father's club, The Graham Texas Golf Club. I borrowed the member's clubs and my obsession with golf began. Today I own numerous sets of custom clubs. I try to replicate Ben Hogan's swing as well as his fashion sense. In 1957, I traveled to Fort Worth, Texas. I planned to purchase my first set of Hogan Clubs on West Pafford Street, the location of the Hogan Club Manufacturing Plant. Playfully, I asked the employee in attendance if I could speak with Ben.

"*Do you mean Mr. Hogan?*" he asked.

"*Yes.*" I said a smile on my lips. The young man asked me to wait and moments later I was standing face to face with my golf hero. Ben and I looked over his stock of clubs; Ben questioned me about certain aspects of my game before settling on a set. I cherished that set of clubs for over 50 years.

Ben Hogan's Famous Swing. USGA Museum

German Gas

My Dad rarely spoke of his service in WWI but I knew that he battled in the trenches in France. Of course, I did not really understand the war. I just knew it had something to do with my Dad gobbling up antacids and gulping down milk to keep his stomach from hurting. I overheard plenty of talk about folks coming back from France or being too yellow to go over there.

My Dad returned from WWI in 1919. His service included a year in France and Germany as an ammunitions man in a machine gun squad. Dad was right there in the trenches.

During WWI the Germans used gas attacks regularly to gain a battlefield advantage. The introduction of trench warfare pitted two armies close enough to each other that they could yell across the lines. But soldiers rarely ventured into the "no man's land" as they would be shot down. In order to injure, kill or debilitate the other side and gain ground, gas was employed. Both sides used a variety of chemical weapons including tear gas, mustard gas, chlorine, and the most deadly phosgene.

Although gas killed only 4% of soldiers in combat, it was the most dreaded and feared weapon. When implemented, a slow-moving gas cloud would travel across to the enemy's trench and crudely and unpredictably wreak havoc. Gas impacted soldiers' lungs by asphyxiating its victim. It burned through and attacked the other internal organs as well. Men would fall to the ground clutching their throats. They would twist and gasp in despair and pain. The crudest type, mustard gas, caused internal and external blisters and burned its way through the skin. Those who did recover were at higher risk of developing cancers or other deadly and painful maladies later in life.

WWI Gas Mask 1917. Library and Archives Canada

These torturous attacks killed some soldiers and injured others. My father's exposure to German gas attacks plagued him with stomach ulcers for the remainder of his life. On a daily basis I watched as he ingested large quantities of milk and antacids. Sometimes the attacks were more serious. I remember the August day in 1927 when Dad left the house to plow the field. I awoke to my Mother nervously glancing out the window toward the field.

"What is it, Mom?" I asked.

"Your Dad should have hitched up the mules by now. I don't see him. Do you see him out there?" I looked out at the field and Dad was

nowhere to be seen. Mother rushed to the barn. To her horror, a pool of blood spread beside the plow and the mules with my Dad collapsed in the center.

Enlisting the neighbors help, my Mother managed to get him into our Chevrolet. At full speed the neighbor drove us the 18 miles to the closest hospital in Olney, Texas.

Having only the memories of a six year old, I can't say with any accuracy how long my Dad was hospitalized. The most vivid image I can think of that terrible time is the quiet yet confident presence of Dr. McFarland. He had the largest hands I had ever seen. Dr. McFarland placed those massive hands on my shoulders and comfort seeped through me. As young as I was I knew that my Dad could die but those hands performed surgery on my Dad and saved his life. Successful stomach or any other kind of surgery represented quite an accomplishment for medicine in 1920s.

Dr. McFarland inspired me. As I heard the sound of Dr. McFarlane's step retreating down the hallway I told my Mother, "*I am going to be a doctor.*"

"*Yes, Jack*", my Mother replied.

"*I really am.*"

"*I know dear.*" She said, and then reminded me of the recent commitment I made to a career in train engineering after hearing a train whistle earlier that week.

Nevertheless, I never forgot Dr. McFarlane. To this day I can picture those firm, consoling hands.

Eventually, my father's stomach issues progressed and he could not physically manage the farm duties. Nine years after his surgery, I dropped out of my sophomore year of high school to work the farm. I was the only child and in those hard times it was the only reasonable alternative.

In my youth, I fortunately never had to plow a field with a team of mules like my father. Dad purchased a tractor before I took over the farm duties. I spent many hours on this vehicle; planting and plowing cotton and corn, pulling the combine to harvest wheat, barley and oats. Neighbors not lucky enough to have their own tractor hired me to assist in their chores. They would fill up the tractor with gas at 15 cents a gallon and pay me for my labor. I made about $2.50 per day.

When I returned to school I was more resolute than ever to avoid the life of a farmer.

Aviation

The same year of dad's surgery another vocation piqued my interest and became my lifelong focus; aviation. My affinity for aviation could be part a product of the times coupled with the stress of my dad's illness. In 1927 Charles Lindbergh electrified the world with his the solo west-to-east conquest of the Atlantic. The dream of flying into the wild blue yonder dominated my thoughts when I was 6 and never left me.

A genetic component may have also come into play. My maternal Uncle, Earl Murray, became a pilot.

Uncle Earl flew a bi-plane with an open cockpit showcasing his skills around the air show circuit. Watching in awe bystanders filled the fairgrounds in county after county. In the fall of 1928, Uncle Earl spryly hopped into the cockpit and readied himself for another amazing performance. Uncle Earl delivered. Then the crowd stared in horror when he turned the plane upside down and his seat belt failed to hold him. Uncle Earl plummeted to his death. Despite this tragedy, I felt compelled to fly.

1920s Bi-Plane. National Museum of the United States Air Force

My even temper and mild mannered character consistently clashed with my attraction to thrills and danger. But I have always had an adventurous side. My best friend, Aubrey McCarthy, had a way of tapping into my wild side. The two of us went off on a couple cross country escapades that made my Mother's hair turn white.

At 16 I bought a Harley Davidson motorcycle for $5 and drove with Aubrey to Shreveport, Louisiana. I found the bike in a scrap heap but it had good tires and still ran. After about 200 miles into the adventure, we had run out of money completely. In order to buy gas and get home, we picked strawberries to earn a few bucks. We purchased used oil from the service stations along the Louisiana Bayous. The gas stations served mostly motor boats instead of cars. We were unaccustomed to sharing the shoreline with alligators. I don't know how long we stayed but I recall how tired, hungry and happy we were to get home. I junked the Harley upon arrival.

Our next trip in 1938 landed us in Seattle, Washington. With no money but plenty of bravado, we set out in a 1928 Model A Ford. After making it through Texas, our first stop was in Clovis, New Mexico. Unlike road trips nowadays, it was common to stop, work, and when you could afford it move on down the road. We picked cotton for several days to make enough money to continue our trip. During our stay in Clovis, Aubrey and I met another broke gentleman who had been discharged from the Navy. He aimed to get back to his home in Seattle. Although Aubrey and I had no plans to travel that far, he talked us into it.

The three of us gradually made our way to Washington State by panhandling, sweeping out warehouses, dumping trash and washing dishes in restaurants. The whole time, our new friend told stories about his tour with the Navy. It was the final push I needed to enlist. The next time I left home, I was on a train to Dallas and sworn into the U.S. Navy.

Joining Up

Baking in my graduation robe, I waited for my name to be called. I wore a newly purchased pair of store-bought slacks and a white button down shirt Mother found for me in town. My small class of 17 graduates gathered outside the Methodist church. I could feel the beam of pride by my parents as I shook the Principal's hand and grasped my diploma. But I drifted miles away envisioning the sea and the movement of the ships I would soon be aboard.

Ever since my return from my cross-country adventure with Aubrey, our New Mexican companion's tales of naval glory filled my head. Then on September 16, 1940, the President signed the Selective Training and Service Act which proclaimed the existence of a limited national emergency and authorized the Navy to increase its personnel strength to 145,000 men. Units newly commissioned to engage in neutrality patrol had to be manned. The Act represented the first peacetime draft in American History. FDR wanted to strengthen unprepared US forces. The act required men 21-36 to register; ultimately 45 million men registered and more than 10 million were inducted between November 1941 and October 1946.

After the graduation ceremony, Aubrey sidled up to me. His hair was slicked back and he had a mischievous grin. *"Going to the river tonight?"* Aubrey asked.

"I have to prepare for my trip. I wish you would come with me." I said. *"Like old times."*

"I can't leave my folks." Aubrey said sheepishly. In truth, I knew he couldn't leave Charmaine, the gas station owner's daughter. Poor Aubrey could never accept that Charmaine only had eyes for Charlie Terry. We shook hands and I left to join my folks.

On April 24, 1940, I pulled on my graduation slacks and shirt, closed up my suitcase and loaded into the car with my parents. As we pulled away, I still thought Aubrey McCarty might come bounding out of the pasture, jump in the car and enlist with me. But Aubrey never materialized. He stayed behind and instead joined the CCCS, one of FDR's New Deal programs.

My parents and I drove 63 miles to the closest Naval Recruiting Station in Wichita Falls, Texas. We walked into the rickety building and my Mother and Dad stepped forward with me. I could see her hand twitch as she reluctantly signed the paperwork. My Dad retreated toward the corner of the small room and watched her sign. My folks probably had serious reservations about their only child enlisting but they stood by as I raised my right hand and was sworn in for duty. My father's grip was firm. My Mother said nothing as she hugged me goodbye.

I boarded the half empty train for Dallas and left my Texas boyhood behind. Upon arrival at the Dallas Naval Recruiting Center, they swore me in a second time. I felt sheer excitement as I boarded the next train heading to San Diego.

I honestly never dreamt I would be involved in World War II. No one did. Despite the increasing fighting in Europe, and the President's Selective Training and Service Act, 1940 enlistees generally didn't believe the War would extend to us. The US public, media and politicians held a deeply isolationist stance in 1939 and 1940. Americans felt bitter about our involvement in the First World War and the majority of the population wished to 'avoid foreign entanglements' and focus on domestic issues. The United States proclaimed its neutrality officially as the Germans marched into Poland in 1939.

The Neutrality Acts had been passed by the Congress in the 1930s, in response to the escalating trouble in Europe and Asia. Isolationism and non-interventionism dominated American opinion following its costly involvement in World War I. US citizens did not want to be tangled again in foreign conflicts. But the Neutrality Acts were poorly constructed even interpreting aggressors and victims equally as "belligerents".

President Roosevelt clearly stated in a Boston campaign speech on October 30, 1940 *"I have said this before, but I shall say it again and again: your boys are not going to be sent into any foreign wars."* The President repeated this sentiment throughout the campaign.

Franklin Roosevelt, President of the United States, 1941. History.com

I do believe, and historians have supported, that as time went on President Roosevelt wanted to join the conflict to help the British survive. But the U.S. population was so steadfastly opposed to war that President Roosevelt could not disregard public sentiment. Instead, he took measures to assist the Allied forces without actually engaging in war.

Prior to the Japanese bombing of Pearl Harbor, journalists probed many of our military leaders and government officials asking *"Do you think Japan would ever attack the United States?"* Without exception their answer was something to the effect of *"No, they would never attempt such a foolish action."*

In order to understand the experiences I was about to encounter in the Pacific as well as later on in my military career in England, one must have a grasp of the causes of World War II, the nations that played a part and the immense geographical expanse of the War.

The Axis armies fought the Allied armies in World War II. The Axis powers included three countries: Germany, Italy and Japan. Great Britain, France, the Soviet Union and the United States along with several smaller countries ultimately comprised the Allied forces

The turmoil leading to World War II began at the end of World War I in 1918. The allied forces, Great Britain, France, the United States and Italy, defeated Germany. Subsequently, the parties signed the Treaty of Versailles which required Germany to take full responsibility for the war and pay $33 billion dollars in reparations. Finding that sum impossible to repay, Germany printed more money, which only increased their problems by creating inflation. In other words, German money was all but worthless.

German's economic problems worsened along with the rest of the world when the Great Depression of 1929 hit the United States then spread globally. In desperation the German people turned to the Nazi Party and its leader, Adolph Hitler.

The fascist Nazi party emphasized extreme patriotism and began strengthening their army. Although this escalating of the German army violated the terms of the Treaty of Versailles, England and France ignored it. This appeasement would lead to further overreaching by Germany.

Hitler aligned himself with Benito Mussolini of Italy and made a pact with the Military Generals who led Japan. Each member of this group, known as the Axis Powers, began to overtake land belonging to other countries. Japan took over China; Italy invaded Ethiopia; and Germany annexed Austria.

In 1938 British and French leaders met with Hitler. In a mistaken attempt to end further aggression, the leaders agreed that Germany could take over parts of Czechoslovakia. The British and French leaders rationalized that the Austrian and Czech lands belonged to Germany before WWI and weren't worth fighting over.

Then, on September 1, 1939, Germany invaded Poland. This "blitzkrieg" or lightening war began WWII. Initially, the Soviet Union was allied with Germany and split possession of Poland with the Germans. But, in 1941, Germany invaded the Soviet Union thus the Soviets transformed into an Allied Force.

The United States had not entered the war, but supplied naval support, weapons and equipment to the British. The United States tried to stop Japan with a trade embargo.

I experienced the devastation of Japan's response to the embargo when they bombed Pearl Harbor on December 7, 1941. The United States declared war on Japan and Italy and Germany declared war on the United States.

Once the United States entered the War, all Americans did their part for the war effort. Henry Ford altered his assembly lines to build for the military. His assembly line was one mile long.

The B-24 had a Davis Wing, which was very narrow, and was too small for a normal sized person to get inside and shoot and buck rivets. Henry Ford went to Galveston, Texas and hired every midget that worked for the Barnum and Bailey and Ringling Brothers circus to work inside the wings. Their size gave them an advantage in assembling planes. Henry Ford produced a B-24 every hour. He built a total of 11,000 aircraft.

The Allied Forces fought World War II in three theaters: the Pacific, France and North Africa. I fought battles in two of these theaters, the Pacific and France.

My Naval career began a short time before the United States entered the War. At that time, the training of recruits for the Navy was carried on at four widely separated establishments, all of which had been in existence since World War I, or before. These stations were in Newport, R.I., Great Lakes, Ill., Norfolk, Va., and San Diego, Calif.

The fourth naval training station, at San Diego, Calif. was established in 1917 during World War I. Originally, the training station consisted of a group of tents in Balboa Park. In 1923, the Navy developed a permanent training station north of the city, overlooking the bay. By 1939, the station had facilities enough to provide accommodations for 5,000 recruits.

As I embarked from Texas for Boot Camp at this facility, I could not contain my excitement. I found a window seat and watched Texas slip away. A distinguished looking gentleman sat across the aisle. He removed his hat and made himself comfortable.

"*Son, you look chipper.*" He said with a smile.

"Yes sir. I am heading to San Diego." I grinned. "*Just joined up.*"

"*Well, you best get some rest. They will keep you on your toes when you arrive, I imagine.*"

Taking his kindly advice, I snuggled into the seat as best I could and let the rhythm of the train lull me into sleep. I awoke in the darkness nauseous with a dull pain in my navel. I twisted and turned trying to ease the pain but it rapidly became more pronounced and seemed to move lower. I tossed in any direction I thought would minimize my discomfort. Suddenly I dashed to the train's bathroom. I vomited for what seemed like an eternity. Dazed, I fumbled out of the restroom compartment. As I moved through the shaking train the floor appeared to roll and I stumbled back for fear I would be sick again. Finally, I progressed to my car and staggered toward my seat. The gentleman stirred.

"*Boy, are you alright? You look like the Dickens.*" Every movement delivered a stabbing pain as he helped settle me back into the wooden seat. "*You are burning up.*" He said.

"*My stomach, I feel terrible*" I confessed, "*I don't know what's happening.*"

As the hours wore on the pain increased and my abdomen swelled. I suffered with every movement. The man sat next to me and tried to offer comfort as we traveled the last few hours.

I waved to the man as I was carried into an ambulance and taken to the naval hospital. I immediately underwent emergency surgery for an appendectomy.

My hospital vigil for my Dad so many years ago haunted me as I visually explored the barren walls of the military hospital. Ever daunting possibility consumed my thoughts. Would I ever realize all the experiences and dreams I had about the Navy?

I felt doomed as the orderlies wheeled me into the operating room. Anesthesia did not exist. The nurse gave me a mild sedative and a spinal injection to deaden the nerves. Bound down onto the operating table I tried to stay as still as possible. I watched the nurses drape a canvas shield over my upper body. It blocked my view of my lower extremities. Although I could not see the doctor plunging his instruments into my abdomen, I felt a thick pinching and random tugging in and outside of my stomach. The clatter of the metal instruments dropping into basins clanged in my ears. The tugging became a painful pull and the doctor announced the appendix was out.

The nurses offered me comfort but a gnawing loneliness coupled with the anxiety of leaving home made for a tough initiation into the Navy. The surgery required three weeks of complete rest and recuperation. I could not do anything but lie in bed. My naval career so far was not what I had anticipated.

In Texas pastures the prickly pear grows abundantly. Cows eat the prickly pears. My last job just prior to joining the Navy was cutting the pears with a long handled shovel, piling pears to dry and then burning them. I had callouses on my hands you would not believe. The Doctor examining me asked, "*What in hell have you been doing son*"?

Finally on the mend, I entered boot camp. The discipline and intimidation began the moment the Company Commander entered the field. Commander Sartorius sternly addressed us as we stood at attention. "*I want you boys to round out those white hats,*" he said referring to the new recruits tendency to try and straighten the stiff, formal white hat issued to us upon arrival. "*I know some of you are pretty salty but most of you still smell like cowshit.*"

We arose at 4 am and filed into the mess hall for breakfast followed by hours and hours of marching. On the drill field we practiced standing at attention or parade rest listening to the company commanders directives. The rest of the day entailed swimming classes, boxing practice and tying knots. I was thankful that my goofy twin Uncles Ewell and Newell had thrown me in Elm Creek when I was three. Although I did not appreciate their gruffness at the time, their version of sink or swim lessons was precisely the preparation I needed. The Navy relentlessly tested our swimming, lifesaving techniques and ability to scramble down cargo nets at an accelerated speed.

We received semaphore training, a method of sending messages ship to ship. It required moving flags in different positions. Each hand position signified a different letter of the alphabet.

After a strenuous day, we laundered our clothes and hung them on a clothes line. Even this simple activity followed guidelines. The clothes had to be tied to the clothes line with a specific knot by a short piece of white line. If the prescribed technique was not followed to the letter, the sailor paid for it on the drill field the following day. I made one mistake and learned my lesson following a day of torture on the field.

Following completion of the two month boot camp training, I applied for and was accepted for additional four month of training in Aviation Machinist Mate School, which was a misnomer. The training focused on Aviation Mechanics.

Jack's Company 32, July 24, 1940. Jack is in the 3rd row, number 7 from left side.

The Navy assigned me to Pearl Harbor. The voyage itself from San Diego to Pearl Harbor was exceptionally treacherous. I ended up on a Navy Tanker, USS Platte, barreling full speed from San Diego to Hawaii. According to Ships Company, the Captain wanted to spend Christmas back in San Diego. Displeased to have to embark on the trip, the Captain kept the vessel at full speed despite the huge storm and 6 million gallons of fuel oil aboard. The heaviness of the ship coupled with its speed resulted in only 3 feet of free board-the distance between the top of the deck and the water.

USS Platte. NavSource.

The sleeping quarters were in the bow of the ship. The bunks consisted of a strip of canvas stretched across a metal frame. The entire company was petrified. When the bow of the ship came up you literally were pinned to the bunk. When the bow dipped you would momentarily be floating in thin air. Obviously, no one slept. The ship's normal speed during such a storm should have been 8 knots. We bashed against the waves and elements at between 12 and 15 knots. Fortunately, the storm lasted only one of the six days we spent at Sea. The experience revealed that even in violent conditions, I was not prone to seasickness.

Pearl Harbor / Assignment in Paradise

Having survived the harrowing voyage, the indescribable Pacific paradise of Hawaii lay before me. Upon arrival in Pearl Harbor, I went straight to VP 23 PBY squadron based on Ford Island. I was instructed to check in with Lieutenant Commander Massie Hughes.

US Navy Rear Admiral Francis Massie Hughes had a grand reputation. He graduated in 1923 from the United States Naval Academy. Hughes served on the Battleship USS Texas and the Cruiser USS Chicago. In 1931 Hughes became a pilot at Pensacola Naval Air Station in Florida.

Captain Francis "Frank" Massie Hughes. Naval Source archives.

I braced myself as I approached his office. In the window I could make out a robust, round faced man seated behind the desk dramatically relaying a story to two other officers.

As I walked in, he stood up and walked around the desk. I immediately relaxed under his generous, welcoming smile.

"*At ease!*" he said in a Tennessee drawl, "*So, Holder, I hear you had a rough arrival in San Diego.*"

"*Yes Sir.*" I replied.

"*This here boy had his appendix out the day he got off the train.*" Lieutenant Commander Hughes said to the two officers. "*Were you in a lot of pain, Holder? I hear it's as bad as giving birth.*" His smile widened. The officers laughed.

"*Not sure about that, Sir. But it was awful painful.*" I said. Lieutenant Commander Hughes' twang and smile won me over instantaneously.

"*Very good, Holder. Head on over to the barracks and get settled. Welcome to Pearl Harbor, Son.*"

Lieutenant Commander Hughes' no nonsense attitude, loyalty and fair treatment of his men captured the admiration and respect of our unit. During my time in Pearl Harbor, Lieutenant Commander Hughes took a shine to me and was on the verge of recommending me for officer training. The paperwork had already been signed by five other officers and was just awaiting his signature. However, when the Japanese arrived on December 7, 1941, I never had the opportunity.

I rarely had contact with Lieutenant Commander Hughes, for my daily duties I reported to Chief Boatswain mate Morris who was in charge of the beaching crew and Swede Segerstrom our leading chief. Morris treated us well and I developed a bond with him. On a few occasions I received invitations for dinner with his family. I enjoyed these diversions from our routine horse playing with his young daughter and son, and enjoying his wife's home cooking.

Swede Segerstrom's more reserved, Scandinavian character made him harder to get to know. I earned his approval quickly. Although he never outwardly praised my work, he would peer down at me from his 6'3" height and give a solemn but appreciative nod.

As a young recruit, I was far from becoming a plane crew member. I worked for four months with the beach crew as my initial assignment. As the PBY aircraft did not have landing gear, the crew needed to attach beaching gear as the plane came out of the water and remove it upon return. This task required 7 men. The main beaching gear required 3 men on either side of the plane and one tail hook person. The tractor pulls the airplane out and the men attach the gear on the way out for maneuvers and remove it upon return.

A short time after my arrival, I became the permanent tail hook (I did not have to go into the water), much to the envy of my fellow beach crew. No one enjoyed submersing themselves in water day after day. I attribute this coveted assignment to Chief Boatswain mate Morris' kinship toward me. I was passed up on the mess cook assignment. Thanks to Chief Boatswain mate Morris.

Otherwise known as the Catalina Flying Boat, PBY Squadrons operated unusually. We did not fly in formation. Consolidated Aircraft built the Catalina Flying Boat in 1935 and the PBY in 1939. PB stands for "patrol bomber" and the Y indicated that Consolidated Aircraft was the manufacturer. The PBY's primary purpose was as a patrol and rescue vehicle. During the war our primary duty was anti-submarine patrol. But this versatile machine could act as a night bomber, convoy protection, anti-submarine patrol, long-range reconnaissance, air/sea rescue, glider tug and even a mail and transport service aircraft.

The PBY's measurements are: 104 feet wing span; 64 feet long; 18 feet high; 17,464 pounds when empty; 15,000 cargo capacity; 18,200 service ceiling; 196 mph maximum speed; 130 mph cruising speed. The plane is equipped with all metal retractable wing floats for take-off and landing. Two Pratt Whitney 9-cylinder 1830 radial air cooled engines power the PBY producing 1200 horse power each.

The Consolidated PBY Catalina was an American flying boat, and later an amphibious aircraft of the 1930s and 1940s produced by Consolidated Aircraft. Courtesy of Consolidated Airplane Corporation.

Generally, each PBY went out alone. In the event of a bombing raid or torpedo attack we could and did go with more than one plane. If we found an enemy target we could either report its location, distance from the nearest base direction of travel and estimated speed. If the submarine was our primary target we made the attack.

Following the attack on Pearl Harbor the PBY played a vital part in winning the war. This aircraft became an integral part of my day to day life and service to the Navy. From July 1942 to January 1943, I flew 34 missions of anti-submarine patrol over Guadalcanal and the Marshall and Gilbert Islands, Savo Islands, Renault, Espirito Santo, New Hebrides and all of the Solomon Islands.

After graduating from beach crew duty, the Navy assigned me to a plane crew as a "1st Mech" or mechanic and a waist hatch gunner for 5-6 months. In October 1940, I received a promotion to Plane Captain. The job entailed the duties required of an Air Force Flight Engineer in addition to the responsibilities for maintaining their assigned aircraft. In other words, I monitored and operated every aspect of the aircraft system and along with the rest of the crew flew training missions and patrols of the outlying islands nearly every day.

Lieutenant Commander Hughes planted himself in the center of the podium for every pre-flight briefing. He waited for complete silence and informed each and every crew member of their route and distance for the day's flight.

Lieutenant Commander Hughes repeated the information received from intelligence as to the location of enemy ships, and subs as well as the weather report. Despite the routine nature of the briefings, Lieutenant Commander Hughes treated each and every one solemnly and thoroughly. We knew exactly the bomb loads, the amount of ammunition and fuel, and precisely how long we could remain airborne.

Our typical training flight routes traveled to and from the Islands of Johnston; Palmyra and all around the Hawaiian Islands; aerial gunnery flights and practice bombing runs. Preparations for training flights and missions entailed study of enemy, primarily Japanese, aircrafts and ships.

Pearl Harbor Prior To 12/7/1941

When I arrived in Pearl we sailors spent our shore leave carousing the streets of Honolulu.

I was partial to a piano joint in Diamond Head. The seasoned piano player hailed from San Francisco and we exchanged stories as he played requests.

Ensign O'Dowd hung around with our squadron for these pub crawls until Navy officials reprimanded him for associating with enlisted men. Lieutenant Commander Hughes in no uncertain terms told him to "change his habits."

Like any young man, I yearned for female companionship. Honolulu's Hotel Street accommodated those needs. When Naval ships came in, the lines at the brothels literally stretched down the block. The men felt no shame passing their afternoons in the lines as Honolulu's citizens passed by to go about their business. It was just a reality of service. The going rate was $3.00 for servicemen.

According to the *The Honest Courtesan, Honolulu Harlots*, July 5, 2011, these were the rules for the prostitutes at the time of the Pearl Harbor attack.

- *She may not visit Waikiki Beach or any other beach except Kailua Beach [across the mountains from Honolulu].*
- *She may not patronize any bars or better class cafes.*
- *She may not own property or an automobile.*
  She may not have a steady "boyfriend" or be seen on the streets with any men.
- *She may not marry service personnel.*
- *She may not attend dances or visit golf courses.*
- *She may not ride in the front seat of a taxicab, or with a man in the back seat.*
- *She may not wire money to the mainland without permission of the madam.*
- *She may not telephone the mainland without permission of the madam.*
- *She may not change from one house to another.*
- *She may not be out of the brothel after 10:30 at night.*

During the Second World War, the demand from servicemen grew so large that most of the cathouses on Hotel Street simply stopped seeing local men altogether. As the prostitutes serviced around 100 men a day, they had to be efficient. Hotel Street developed a "bull pen" system. The cathouse matron weeded out the unsavory characters and took the $3 from appropriate customers. Each man received a poker chip, and then waited for a room. While he undressed he could hear the girl in the next room through the make-shift "wall". When it was his turn, she came in, collected the chip, examined him for signs of venereal disease, washed him and did her work.

The Honest Courtesan, Honolulu Harlots July 5, 2011

I frequently visited a beautiful redhead from San Francisco. These encounters cost me $3. Despite the rules, she snuck me to her apartment on the island on occasion.

But after the bombing, the pubs and cat houses vanished. After the attack, these young ladies acted as volunteer nurses tending to the wounded. Soon afterward they shipped back to San Francisco on the December 20th evacuation transport on the *Lurline*.

Pearl Harbor's jovial atmosphere disappeared. All inhabitants maintained continued vigilance from that day to the end of the War.

Observation of Destruction

    Just prior to December 7, a British heavy cruiser docked in Pearl Harbor and tied to a mooring on Ford Island. It had just escaped from a battle in the southwest Pacific.

    I boarded the freshly devastated ship walked amid bulkheads (walls) saturated in blood and fresh human remains. Many wounded sailors in agony filled the compartments. Body parts lay scattered all over the ship's decks. The stench was unbearable. It was my first exposure to the smell of blood and death. Apparently the ship had only one doctor and no nurses. Many of the crew wore slings on their arms and had patches covering their faces and eyes. Some sailors stumbled around on make-shift crutches. The Captain had shrapnel wounds on his upper body, chest and shoulders.

    The ship stayed only long enough to refuel and load supplies and food. I watched as it sailed away. I am not sure whether the ship stayed afloat and made it back to England.

    Before seeing the battered ship, I heard about a British battleship which was presumably unsinkable, the H.M.S. Hood. While traveling near the Philippines it fell under the attack of Japanese dive bombers. The Japanese sunk the ship within 5 minutes. These threatening warnings came just months before December 7.

Meanwhile, the political climate between Japan and the United States became increasingly tense. In response to Japanese advances in French Indochina and China, the United States, England and the Netherlands, cut off all oil supplies to Japan. These countries had provided 90% of Japan's oil. The oil embargo threatened to grind the Japanese military machine to a halt Japan knew its refusal to leave China would ultimately result in war with the United States. The Japanese were determined to strike first. Admiral Isoroku Yamamoto, the supreme Japanese Naval Commander, decided it was imperative to knock out the main American fleet immediately. Yamamoto's fleet approached within 200 miles of Hawaii without being detected.

A Day That Will Live In Infamy

On Saturday December 6, 1941 I had no military requirements or flying scheduled. I relaxed, played racquetball and enjoyed an afternoon nap. I dined on pork chops, green beans and a nice green salad. For dessert I strolled over to the canteen for my ice cream, a treat I continue to enjoy. Oblivious that the next day my life and the lives of all Americans would change forever.

My routine in Pearl Harbor dictated that every 4th day I had "duty" which mandated staying on board. I woke up at 0500 and completed my daily stretching exercises. After showering and shaving, I dined on the Navy's shipwrecked ham and eggs in lay terms, and a large orange juice. It was just an ordinary morning.

At 7:55 a.m. on December 7, 1941, my section had just fallen in for muster in our hangar. I had duty, but other members of my squadron planned on heading to church, Waikiki beach or their chosen Sunday recreational activity. As our section leader began calling roll, we heard a screaming aircraft then a terrible explosion. We ran outside.

The neighboring VP-21 hangar had been hit by the first bomb dropped on Ford Island. It was engulfed in smoke and flames.

Overhead we saw several planes with the rising sun insignia. We immediately realized what was happening. Someone in our section knew that there was a sewer line being constructed behind the hangar.

He yelled "*Let's go to the ditch.*" About 20 of us followed him and jumped in the ditch. As we ran, I looked up and saw a Japanese plane circle and head straight for us. The pilot saw us, and as he approached I helplessly clung to the side of the ditch sure this was the end of us all. I could see the expression on his face – wide-eyed with an expansive toothy grin. In shock, I momentarily froze.

The plane spat tongues of machine gun fire. Bullets landed all around me. The machine gun fire hit the dirt piled up beside the ditch missing us by a mere 3 feet.

I do not know how long we clustered in the ditch. We waited until the first wave of the attack was over. I remember my hands clenching my shipmate's shoulders. Thoughts raced through my head, *God don't let me die in this ditch*. Aside from the occasional murmur, we didn't speak. Our fear was intense, but our determination unrelenting. If I was destined to die in this ditch, I would go down fighting.

PBY Hangars. Sailors working to save planes

When I left the ditch I saw the devastation of the PBY hangars, VP-23 and VP-21 and all aircraft engulfed in smoke and flames.

It was the most devastating sight I have ever seen and will never forget.

I knew I was in the middle of the beginning of something devastating and the fear that engulfed me was real. The fear soon turned to adrenaline of wanting to know what to do and the excitement of action came over me and turned to 'what can we do to fight back.'

I immediately caught sight of our squadron Captain Hughes, still wearing his red pajamas, running down the road waiving his 45 caliber and shouting *"Shoot those Sons-of-bitches!"*

Ford Island. Sailors watch USS Shaw explode

While the VP-21 was engulfed in flames I was directed, to the VP-23 hangar by the leading Chief to ready the squadron commander's plane for flight. The engines were buttoned up, plane was rolled out, refueled, loaded with two 1000 lb. bombs. The captain and his crew flew 19 hours searching for the Japanese Task Force and found nothing.

Only two weeks prior my unit had flown these planes in from San Diego. Fortunately, the VP-21 squadron happened to be in the Philippines on advanced base training.

That was not the only lucky happenstance for the United States. The Japanese launched this surprise attack against the US Forces on a Sunday in hopes of catching the entire fleet in port.

Vice Admiral Nagumo Chuichi.

But the Aircraft Carriers and one of the Battleships were not in port. The USS Enterprise was returning from Wake Island; The USS Lexington was shipping aircraft to Midway; the USS Saratoga and USS Colorado were being repaired in the mainland. Admiral Nagumo. Japanese Flight Admiral, ignored Japanese intelligence reports that the carriers were absent and went forward with the attack.

Isoroku Yamamoto

Following the raid on Pearl Harbor Yamamoto was congratulated on his success. He said, *"I have traveled the United States they are a very industrious nation and I am afraid we have awaken a sleeping giant."*

Seventy-five minutes had elapsed between the first and second waves. Our first task was to separate the damaged from the undamaged aircraft.

The Japanese continued the attack with their force of 6 carriers and 423 aircraft. They launched the first wave of a two-wave attack from approximately 200 miles North of Oahu. The first wave consisted of 183 fighters, dive bombers and torpedo bombers. They struck the fleet in Pearl Harbor, Ford Island, Hickman Field,

Kaneohe and EWA. Next, 167 Japanese aircraft attacked the same targets during the second wave.

When the second wave was over I took a long look at the devastation. The Arizona engulfed in smoke and flames, listing heavily and sinking. The Destroyer Shaw was hit by bombs and torpedoed in floating dry dock across the bay from our hangar. The Arizona, West Virginia, Tennessee and Nevada, California, Maryland and Oklahoma one behind the other had all been hit by bombs and torpedoes. One thousands sailors remain entombed in the Arizona. The Japanese torpedoed and sank the Oklahoma. It turned turtle up and 429 sailors perished. Although the Arizona and Oklahoma were a total loss, the other ships were raised, repaired and returned to duty.

The Pennsylvania was docked abreast the naval Shipyard. The Utah was on the opposite side of Ford Island.

Badly damaged, the Nevada still tried to get under way. It managed to make it to the other side of Ford Island but was sinking so its sailors purposely ran it aground. Like the California it was later repaired.

The flames and wreckage surrounded and suffocated me with grief but I had little time to review the damage. The raid continued for a five-hour period as six carriers sent two waves of 350 dive-bombers, torpedo planes and fighters. US damages escalated to eight battleships, ten smaller warships, and 230 aircraft;

2,400 American soldiers and sailors were killed. Two of the battleships were a total loss but the other 6 were raised and repaired.

Having completely taken the U.S. by surprise, Japan suffered comparatively miniscule losses. American forces shot down a mere 29 planes.

After the attack, measures to defend our homeland went immediately into place. Troops took positions around the entire perimeter of the main Hawaiian Islands. General Walter C. Short declared Martial Law effective immediately. Additionally, he announced that he was taking over the Hawaiian Territorial Government. Blackouts, curfews, censorship and any other restriction deemed necessary by the Army came into place. The Army took over the airports. All private planes were grounded. Troops placed barricades at shore in order to thwart a possible Japanese landing.

Active Machine Gun Pits at Ford Island

By early evening, sand bag machine gun pits had been constructed all around Ford Island. The pits housed three men. Along with my two shipmates, I occupied one of them for 3 days and nights. We watched and waited. Never sure when and if a third wave of Japanese might materialize from the sea or sky. The complete surprise exposed our vulnerability. Now all we could do is alternating sleeping, eating bologna sandwiches and standing watch and fighting mosquitoes.

There would be no third wave. Despite Commander Minoru Genda's, the chief planner of the raid, strong urging to send Japanese forces to airstrike the shore facilities, oil storage tanks, and submarines, and to hunt down the American carriers they believed to be nearby, Commander Nagumo decided not to risk further action.

Commander Minoru Genda. National Archives

Of course, hunkered down in the machine gun pit we could have no way of knowing they were not returning. In our minds, every aircraft or ship noise sounded like the Japanese returning. Enveloped in darkness, unable to know what was happening outside the walls of sand, every plane engine evoked a surge of alertness and fear. After 72 hours the pit reeked of our sweat and anxiety.

While I stood watch in the pit, other sailors left Pearl Harbor to pursue the Japanese. Most of the cruisers and destroyers took a southern course. The Japanese had retreated to the North so no contact was made.

Approximately two dozen naval fighter pilots took off from the USS Enterprise in pursuit of the Japanese attack fleet. Six of the fighters were sent to Oahu and were subjected to friendly fire from panicked American ground troops. Three of the six pilots were shot down and killed. Two landed on Ford Island and the final plane ran out of fuel causing the pilot to parachute down near Barbers' Point. Ensign Ruark and his crew flew to Palmyra, about 700 miles Southwest of Pearl Harbor. He was part of our PBY squadron. Upon return trying to land in Pearl Harbor in total darkness, the plane crashed into the water. US Naval personnel found the plane the next day. All the crew died still strapped to their seats.

For the Japanese, reaching Pearl Harbor for the initial strike had been no small feat. They had to learn how to refuel at sea (a technique the US Navy already had worked out); to sink all those ships they used their superb electric torpedoes and perfected shallow-water bombing tactics. The Japanese had good equipment, talented pilots, total ambush, and an ingenious plan. While everyone suspected the US would be dragged into the war, none of us stationed in Pearl Harbor expected an attack.

Despite later rumors, there was no advance knowledge of the Japanese plan. The commanders had been complacent about routine defensive measures. Even if the defense had been more alert, the surprise and overwhelming power of the Japanese strike probably would have been decisive.

On the fourth day, we returned to the barracks and found all our lockers broken into to retrieve white clothing for bandages.

The Navy issued a postcard to all personnel to send home with one of two messages: *"I am wounded"* or *"I am ok."* We could say nothing more.

During my remaining time on Pearl Harbor I heard many accounts of what other sailors experienced on that fateful morning.

As most of the first raid was on the hangars and barracks, guys in those places lay helplessly behind or under flimsy shelters while bomb splinters or machine gun bullets and debris flew around like hell.

Like me, others spent a hell of a night in the machine gun pit, watching, sleeping, and fighting mosquitoes. Cold and rainy we stewed with rumors of Japanese raiding parties.

On some ships, men reported rushing for the guns on board that didn't have their firing pins installed. The men had to put them in. Then they discovered that the ammunition ready lockers and magazines were locked and the keys could not be found. They had to cut off the locks with bolt cutters. When they could finally fire, they couldn't secure hits. Frustrated and desperate, they watched the torpedoed and bombed battleships enveloped in smoke and plumes of water.

Fourteen months later, I returned home for a short leave. I knocked on the door and shouted *"A sailor out here wants to see you."* Gruffly, my Dad shouted *"You better get in this house!"* With tears in her eyes, my Mother handed me the *"I'm OK."* postcard. My parents had received the postcard on December 17, 1941, nine days after they became aware of the bombing via radio reports. My Dad tried to calm my hysterical Mother. But for those seemingly endless days of not knowing, Mother cried inconsolably and stayed on her knees promising God that if he spared her son's life she would devote the rest of hers to the church. My Mother kept that vow and converted from the Methodist Church to the Church of Christ. She served the church unfailingly from the receipt of that postcard until her death.

Pearl Harbor came as a surprise to the US forces but the Japanese had planned the assault for 12 years. The preparations for a raid on Pearl Harbor included 2 years practicing on a miniature replica of Pearl Harbor. Every Japanese pilot knew exactly what their target was and where it would be.

Prior to the bombing of Pearl Harbor, the Navy had enlisted men who were aircraft pilots; AP-3C (Aircraft Pilot third class), AP-2C, AP-1C or Chief AP. Following December 7, all enlisted pilots were immediately advanced to officer status. Typically, an AP-3C became an Ensign; an AP-2C an Ensign or a Lieutenant Junior Grade (Lt J.G.). Our leading chief, Swede Segerstrom, advanced to Lieutenant Commander and Lieutenant Commander Hughes was advanced to Captain.

The promotions were particularly appropriate as Swede had acted as the chief fighter pilot for a squadron of enlisted men that had become so proficient they far outclassed the officer squadrons.

Aftermath

After the Pearl Harbor attack, President Roosevelt called his military staff together and directed them to devise a plan to bomb Tokyo. The advisors proclaimed the idea was impossible as the American forces did not have aircraft with that capability. Roosevelt struggled to his feet and said *"Do not tell me it's impossible."*

They called for Lieutenant Colonel Jimmie Doolittle, who would later become General Doolittle. His orders included selecting a group of capable pilots and began training for short take-offs and landings in the B-25 Mitchell Bomber. Doolittle gathered his pilots and informed them he could not tell them the purpose of their mission, but they may not return. He told them to step forward if they still wanted to participate. Without exception, the pilots stepped forward.

The B-25s were stripped of armor and extra fuel tanks were installed. After extensive training, on April 2, 1942, the group moved onto the USS Hornet and told their mission was to bomb Tokyo. In addition, Doolittle instructed the pilots that their aircrafts had to be airborne in 457 feet (457 feet was the flight deck length). If they take 458, they would be dead.

The plan hit a snag when on April 18, 1942 picket boats spotted the US Naval Task force 650 miles from Japan. Knowing their position had been reported, Admiral Bull Halsey turned the

USS Enterprise and USS Hornet into the wind at flank speed. The USS Hornet launched 16 B-25 bombers. Their plan to reach their targets then fly another 1100 miles to destinations in China fell short 250 miles as a result of the early launch. Seventy-four of the 80 Raiders survived. One crewman was killed during bail out, 2 died in crashes and 8 were captured and three were executed.

    According to several sources the Doolittle Raid, also known as the Tokyo Raid, on 18 April 1942, was an air raid by the United States on the Japanese capital Tokyo and other places on Honshu Island during World War II, the first air raid to strike the Japanese Home Islands. It demonstrated that Japan itself was vulnerable to American air attack, served as retaliation for the Japanese attack on Pearl Harbor on 7 December 1941, and provided an important boost to U.S. morale while damaging Japanese morale. The raid was planned and led by Lieutenant Colonel James "Jimmy" Doolittle, U.S. Army Air Forces.

USAAF B-25B bomber lines up for takeoff from USS Hornet *(CV-8), on the morning of 18 April 1942. Official U.S. Navy Photograph, from the collections of the Naval Historical Center.*

The Japanese planned the attack on Midway Island in retaliation for the April 18 bombing of Tokyo. Admiral Yamamoto's Japanese Navy suffered embarrassment from the mid-April raid on Japan's home islands and at the Battle of Coral Sea in early May. Yamamoto wanted to catch and destroy the US Pacific Fleet's aircraft carrier striking forces. Fortunately for the United States, strong leadership foiled his plan.

Leadership In The Pacific

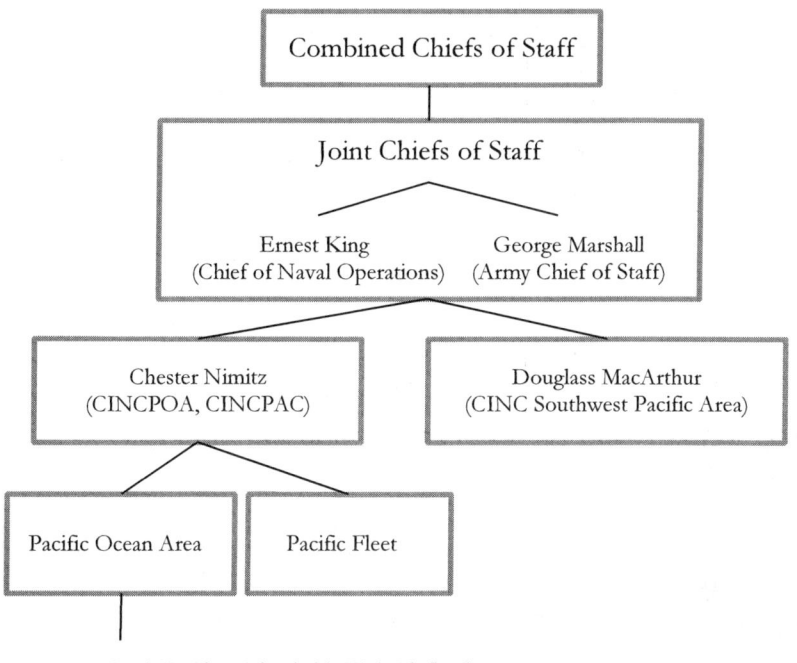

```
                    ┌─────────────────────────┐
                    │ Combined Chiefs of Staff│
                    └─────────────────────────┘
                                │
                    ┌─────────────────────────┐
                    │  Joint Chiefs of Staff  │
                    │                         │
                    │  Ernest King      George Marshall
                    │ (Chief of Naval   (Army Chief of Staff)
                    │   Operations)           │
                    └─────────────────────────┘
                         │              │
            ┌────────────────────┐   ┌────────────────────────┐
            │  Chester Nimitz    │   │  Douglass MacArthur    │
            │ (CINCPOA, CINCPAC) │   │ (CINC Southwest Pacific Area)
            └────────────────────┘   └────────────────────────┘
              │          │
    ┌──────────────┐ ┌──────────────┐
    │Pacific Ocean │ │ Pacific Fleet│
    │    Area      │ │              │
    └──────────────┘ └──────────────┘
            │
```

North Pacific – Theobald, Kinkaid, fletcher
Central Pacific
South Pacific – Ghormley, Halsey, Newton, Calhoun

Provided by several sources to outline the Combined Chiefs of Staff for WWII

Admiral Chester Nimitz (1885-1966). Official U.S. Navy Photograph, from the collections of the Naval Historical Center.

My admiration for Admiral Nimitz began while I served under his command during the War and has extended through my life. A mild mannered Texan like me, Nimitz was the Commander in Chief of the Pacific Fleet from 1941 through the end of the war. The Allied forces' Pacific victory stemmed from the combined wisdom and leadership of Admiral Nimitz and the more colorful and notorious Douglas MacArthur.

Born in Texas in 1885, Chester W. Nimitz served in World War I as chief of staff to the commander of the U.S. Atlantic submarine force. In 1939, he became chief of the Bureau of Navigation of the U.S. Navy. After the Japanese attack on Pearl Harbor, Nimitz rose to Commander in Chief of the Pacific Fleet. In 1944, he was promoted to Fleet Admiral.

Despite the fact that Nimitz was not a Senior Admiral, FDR, as Secretary of the Navy, had opportunity to observe Nimitz. FDR knew first hand of Nimitz' skill and intelligence.

The Allied victory in the Pacific resulted from the leadership of two very different men. The boisterous, show boating MacArthur led through intimidation while Nimitz approached leadership in a relaxed manner. Nimitz emphasized the importance of collaboration and cooperation.

According to historian Ronald Spector, it's hard to imagine two people more different: *"While MacArthur was a forceful and colorful personality, a man of dramatic gestures and rhetoric, Nimitz was soft-spoken and relaxed, a team player, a leader by example rather than exhortation."* Chester Nimitz had an unlikely path to success in the naval ranks.

Although his Granddad served in the Navy, Nimitz initially sought an appointment to West Point. Discovering the appointments had been taken, he reluctantly applied to the Naval Academy. Nimitz did well but nearly tanked his career when he beached a ship under his command. Somehow his career survived that snafu.

Nimitz's first tour was an assignment to the battleship Ohio. The tour predominantly focused on Japan and the Orient. Nimitz even had an introduction to Admiral Togo while in Japan. Admiral Togo would construct the Japanese navy that would become his foe.

Nimitz became an expert in the emerging area of submarine warfare. He instructed Naval Cadets about the subject in 1912. During WWI, he served in the Atlantic sub force. Later, he was instrumental in the building of the submarine base at Pearl Harbor.

His most practical knowledge and expertise derived from the advanced courses he took at the Naval War College in 1922. Their exercises consistently pitted them against the Japanese. Nimitz stated that after completing those courses, nothing that happened in the Pacific at the start of WWII was strange or unexpected. Citing Nimitz invaluable knowledge of the Japanese region, Secretary Frank Knox gave Nimitz command of the Pacific Fleet only days after the Pearl Harbor travesty.

As considerable as his tactical skills were, perhaps Nimitz's greatest gift was his leadership ability. Naval historian Robert Love writes that Nimitz possessed *"a sense of inner balance and calm that steadied those around him."* He also *"had the ability to pick able subordinates and the courage to let them do their jobs without interference. He molded such disparate personalities as the quiet, introspective Raymond A. Spruance and the ebullient, aggressive William F. Halsey, Jr. into an effective team."*

Of course, these same qualities helped ease Nimitz's relationship with MacArthur, no small feat given the amount of coordination called for between their two services. And it's fortunate that Nimitz did not share MacArthur's need for publicity; even the vast Pacific would not have been big enough for two great military leaders. Journalist Robert Sherrod, who spent time in both of their headquarters, said that *"the Admiral was frequently the despair of his public relations men; it simply was not in him to make sweeping statements or to give out colorful interviews."*

Midway The War's Pivotal Battle

Aerial view of Midway

Admiral Nimitz knew there would be retaliation after Doolittle's raid. He just didn't know where.

In anticipation of a retaliatory mission, Admiral Nimitz placed intelligence forces on high alert. Intelligence honed in on coded messages containing two letter abbreviations "AF" and "AO". The rest of the code had been broken. Intelligence had narrowed these designations to signify either Midway or the Aleutian Islands and the location of the next Japanese target. Strategically, the Japanese wanted to create military footholds on the islands standing between the United States and their homeland. Both Midway and the Aleutians fit the bill.

In order to reveal the meaning of these two-letter codes, our Chief of Intelligence had devised a plan to send an un-coded message regarding a fresh water condenser failure on Midway. Admiral Nimitz said send it. The Japanese took the bait and sent their own message relaying to their forces that "AF" had a fresh water condenser failure.

Admiral Nimitz sent a small task force to the Aleutians as a diversion. The Japanese fell for it and Japanese Fleet Admiral Yamamoto advised his forces that the US was headed for the Aleutians and we will now take Midway. Meanwhile, Admiral Nimitz sent the main task force to Midway; the carriers to one location and the other ships to another.

My squadron, VP-23, left Pearl Harbor on May 31, 1942 for Midway to search for Japanese forces. On the third day of patrol we found them. The Japanese were cruising 600 miles away and moving toward Midway under a weather front. Another PBY, 7 degrees to our left, first reported the sighting. We then flew to their position and saw the same Armada: 4 carriers, battleships, cruisers, destroyers, submarines and troop ships. They proceeded in anticipation of occupying Midway.

The attack on Midway began June 4, 1942 as carrier dive bombers and fighters struck the island. Unlike the surprise attack on Pearl Harbor, US Forces had prepared a defense.

On June 4, 1942 at 0400 we were airborne carrying four 500 pound bombs. At 0545 a PBY reported many planes 150 miles away and destined for Midway. Only seven minutes later, my aircraft sighted two aircraft carriers traveling toward Midway and still under a weather front. The carriers would reach Midway in 180 miles.

Burning Oil Tank on Sand Island, June 4, 1942

June 4 at 0645 the Japanese forces struck the Midway atoll with fighters and dive bombers striking the seaplane hangar, fuel tanks, the mess hall, gallery, command post on Sand Island. The powerhouse on Eastern Island also suffered slight damage. As much of Midway comprised of underground bunkers, the U.S. Marines attempted to defend the island with 27 Brewster Buffalo Fighters, the American counter-part to the Japanese Zero Fighter. Only seven Buffalos survived and those incurred severe damage. Of the three runways on Eastern Island, two were destroyed. The

Japanese left the remaining intact in hopes of utilizing it for their purposes in the future.

Mitsubishi A6M3 Zero Model

At sea, the Japanese Zeke (the plane name *Zero* and was adopted by the Allied Forces) and anti-aircraft force from the Japanese fleet annihilated the reported attacks from our American torpedo and scout bombers. Torpedo squadron 8 from the USS Hornet launched 45 torpedo bombers against Japanese ships. Only 5 of these aircraft survived.

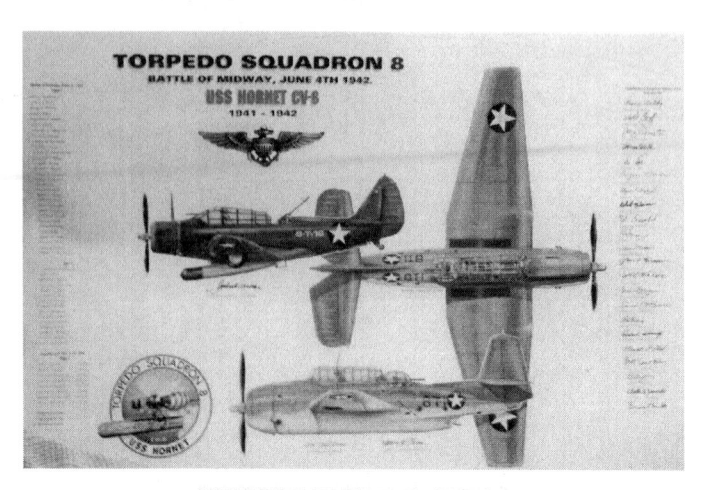

USS Hornet Torpedo Bomber

Fortunately, most installations, including all living quarters, were underground. During the first two hours of battle, the United States stood on the losing side. But the tide was about to turn.

Following the raid, Admiral Nagumo received information that the surface damage was slight and wanted to rearm all aircraft with bombs and restrike the island. Fleet Commander Admiral Yamamoto disagreed, wanting to rearm with torpedoes and strike our ships. When our dive bombers struck, the Japanese were in the process of removing bombs and rearming with torpedoes.

*Rear Admiral Clarence Wade McClusky, Jr., USN
1902 – 1976. Official U.S. Navy Photograph, from the collections of the Naval Historical Center.*

Three squadrons of SBD Dauntless dive bombers led by Commander Max Leslie and Lieutenant Commander Wade McClusky had been searching for the Jap forces for two hours. Despite running low on fuel, McClusky pressed on and only moments later he spotted the white wake of a fast moving Japanese destroyer. McClusky said, *"That destroyer has to be racing to join the main fleet. We will follow it."*

SBD Dauntless Dive Bombers

Diving from 20,000 feet and aided by the Japanese fighters low altitude in order to defend against torpedo planes, the dive bombers inflicted sufficient damage to sink all three carriers: the Kagi, Soryu and the Akagi, which was Admiral Nagumo's flag ship and the pride of the Japanese empire.

Our bomb strikes caused their bombs and torpedoes to explode. In addition, the fuel trucks on the flight deck caught fire turning the entire deck into an inferno.

Commander, Central Pacific Force, U.S. Pacific Fleet Informal portrait photograph, taken 23 April 1944. Official U.S. Navy Photograph, now in the collections of the U.S. National Archives.

Admiral Spruance conferred with Admiral Nimitz characterizing the turn of events as a good day and wondering whether the destruction of three carriers was enough. Admiral Nimitz replied *"Hell, no. I want the fourth carrier."* The US Forces in fact stalked and sank the fourth carrier, the Hiryu, but in turn suffered the loss of The Yorktown.

Late afternoon we spotted a Japanese submarine attempting to submerge. All hatches were closed with no one on deck. We dropped the first bomb near the tail of the sub, second bomb right behind the conning tower. We made 6 circles watching the debris surface.

My squadron lost radio contact with Midway. Having no idea how our side had fared, we had an option to return to Midway or set down at sea. We dropped our two remaining bombs unarmed, set down at sea, and threw out a sea anchor. We floated all night unaware of the day's results.

Grasping the sleeping bag in my cockpit, I climbed on top of the wing and strapped myself to the plane's antennae. I had just flown 13 hours in the battle of Midway Island. Having no idea whether our side was victorious, I fell into a paralyzing sleep. Tomorrow, I would discover our fate and the fate of the American troops in one of the major turning points in WWII.

At sunrise, we finally made radio contact with Midway. To our relief, our side had emerged triumphant. Advised of a destroyer at the French Frigate Shoals loaded with aviation fuel, we took navigational shots, determined our position and flew to the Shoals. After refueling we returned to Pearl Harbor.

Those with limited knowledge of World War II may not recognize the significance of The Battle of Midway. Despite the relatively small amount of men and arms as compared to countless other battles, it was arguably the most important battle of the war. Prior to this victory, the Japanese possessed naval superiority over the U.S. Afterwards, the adversaries became essentially equal and the Americans could take the offensive.

Upon being advised that the fourth Carrier had been sunk, Admiral Nimitz released the following message:

"To you who have participated in the Battle of Midway today you have written a glorious page in our history. I am proud to be associated with you. I estimate that another day of all-out effort on your part will complete the defeat of the enemy."

Even as a participant at Midway, I could not foresee the stunning and overwhelming ramifications of the battle's outcome. Japanese Admiral Yamamoto moved on Midway in order to draw out and destroy the U.S. Pacific aircraft carrier striking forces. Admiral Yamamoto theorized that if Japan could abolish Midway's defenses, attack the surrounding islands they could establish a geographically desirable base. The aptly named Midway Islands were located at the midpoint between Japan and Hawaii. Such a position could cripple the American Pacific Naval Fleet.

Fortunately, Admiral Nimitz' superior communications intelligence afforded the United States the opportunity to ambush the Japanese. Had we lost Midway, the negative domino effect would have been fatal to our cause. For example, the 1942 Guadalcanal invasion would not have occurred thus re-opening the Japanese threat to Australia. As a result, Australia would withdraw troops from North Africa. In all likelihood, Australia would have been neutralized and the American presence there eliminated. Hence, MacArthur's return to the Philippines would have been thwarted and American submarines would not have the Australian bases to disrupt Japanese shipping.

Obviously the Hawaiian Islands would be fully exposed to invasion. The logical extension from there would be our western shores. With such threats to our homeland, the US would have been compelled to curtail our European forces. The implications of a loss at Midway are mind boggling.

Speaking of Midway, Winston Churchill stated "This memorable American victory was of cardinal importance, not only to the United States but to the Whole Allied cause…At one stroke, the dominant position of Japan in the Pacific was reversed." In a more chilling description of events, Admiral Halsey relayed that had we lost Midway, it would have prolonged the war many months and a loss of Midway coupled with a loss of Guadalcanal, we could have lost the war.

Guadalcanal/ Admiral Bull Halsey

After the Pearl Harbor attack, I not only participated in the Battle of Midway Island, but also Marshall and Gilbert, Tulagi, Santa Cruz, Renault, Stewart and Savo Islands.

Guadalcanal played an integral part in the war as the series of islands in the vicinity would act as stopping points between Japan and the United States. That area, in the South Pacific, contained innumerable small islands. Some were inhabited, others were not. In order to effectively wage war, the planes had to hop from island to island in order to refuel.

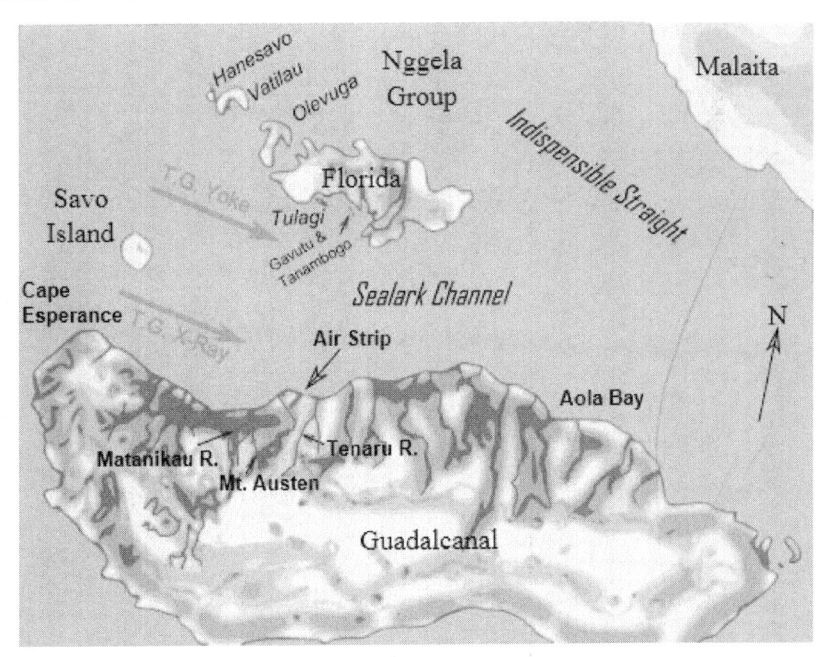

Routes of Allied amphibious forms for landing on Guadalcanal and Tulgai, 7 August, 1942

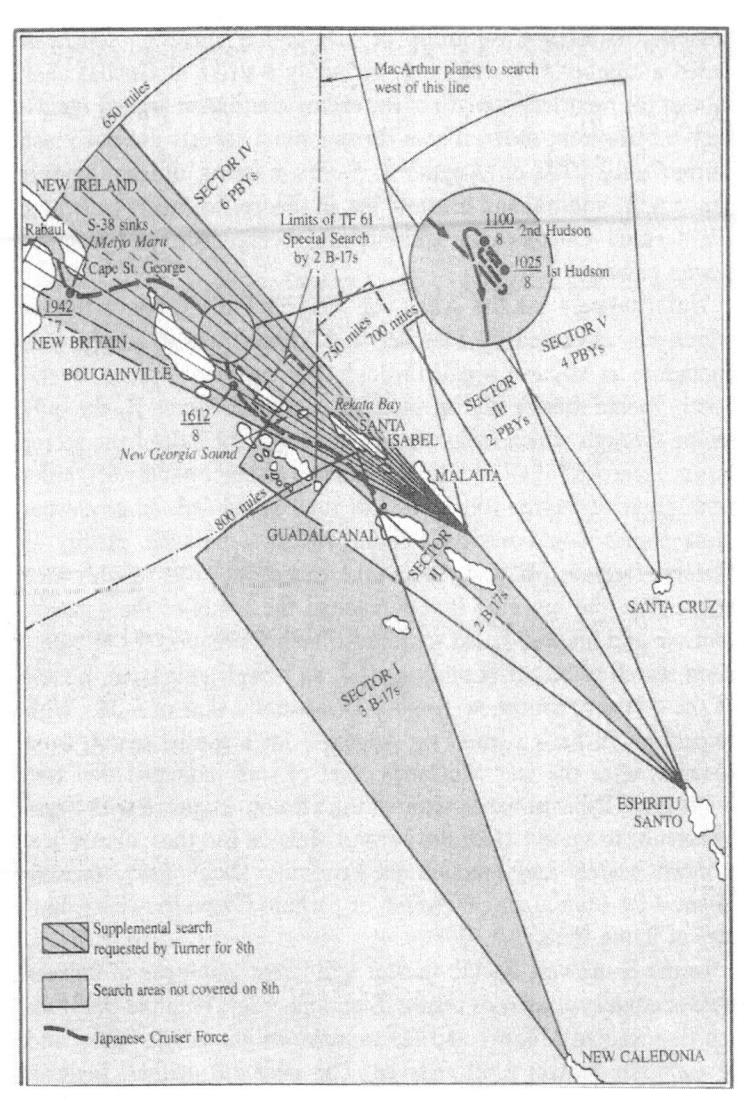

Mikawa's Approach and McCain's' Air-Search Plan

On July 1, 1942, our squadron VP-23 moved to Noumea New Caledonia and began anti-submarine patrol over Guadalcanal and all the Solomon Islands. Our flight crew consisted of 8 men, 5 of which were enlisted men. Every 5th night I spent aboard the aircraft. For 6 months I patrolled over and around Guadalcanal. Only 25 miles in diameter, Guadalcanal rests 3500 miles southwest of Pearl Harbor and 600 miles from Australia.

On October 15, 1942, my squadron, along with the Seaplane Tender USS Curtiss, moved to Espírito Santo.

A seaplane tender provides facilities for operating seaplanes. The USS Curtiss had sustained damages during the attack on Pearl Harbor after a dive bomber dove into one of its topside cranes and other Japanese bombs exploded causing damage in the engine room. The Curtiss lost 20 men at Pearl Harbor. After one month of repairs, the seaplane tender Curtiss was completely mended and went on to serve our squadron.

USS Curtiss (AV-4) Off San Diego, California, during the later 1940s or early 1950s. Official U.S. Navy Photograph, from the collections of the Naval Historical Center.

Vice Admiral Richard Ghormley was the commander of all the Guadalcanal forces. The Vice Admiral had a reputation as a planner who kept his eyes open and his mouth shut. But, this man had never actually been on the island. Things were bleak and we were definitely losing the battle in the South Pacific.

On October 15, 1942, Ghormley sent a letter of resignation to Admiral Nimitz. It read *"My forces are totally inadequate to meet this situation."* Nimitz believed Ghormley an intelligent and dedicated officer but not tough enough to face this crisis.

Vice Admiral Robert L. Ghormley. Official U.S. Navy Photograph, now in the collections of the National Archives.

In October 1942, Admiral Nimitz sent Admiral Halsey to relieve Ghormley. Admiral "Bull" Halsey embodied the stereotype of a street brawler, craving action. His reputation as a no-nonsense, strapping, and resilient character fit the bill.

At Espirito Santo, I had the pleasure of shaking his hand when he came aboard the USS Curtiss.

Fleet Admiral William Frederick Halsey, Jr., USNR 1882 – 1959. Official U.S. Navy Photograph, from the collections of the Naval Historical Center.

I consider Admiral "Bull" Halsey my hero. I believe Halsey and the infamous General George Patton could have been brothers; they thought and acted alike and God help us we needed more like them.

I am providing some infamous quotes to give the reader an insight into the charisma of the Admiral:

In the early 1930s Americans sold scrap iron like crazy and the Japanese were buying it. While passing a San Francisco shipyard and spotting a Japanese freighter being loaded, Halsey said to his son, *"We will get this back in the form of bullets"*.

Emperor Hirohito of Japan rode a beautiful white stallion. At the beginning of the war Halsey said *"I will ride that son of a bitch down Main Street in Tokyo."*

Early in the Pacific conflict, Halsey visited General MacArthur and told him *"You are a smart General but you are glory happy, we need to work together to end this conflict."* After the war, MacArthur said the Pacific Ocean without Halsey will never be the same; it will just be another Ocean.

From 1941-1945 Admiral Halsey commanded the task force centered on the carrier USS Enterprise in a series of raids against Japanese-held targets. He was made commander, South Pacific Area and led the Allied forces over the course of the Battle for Guadalcanal (1942–43) and the fighting up the Solomon chain (1942–45). In 1943 he was made commander of the Third Fleet, the post he held through the duration of hostilities.

USS Enterprise. Photograph from the Bureau of Ships Collection in the U.S. National Archives

Just prior to the Battle of Midway, Halsey lay in the Pearl Harbor Naval Infirmary suffering from a severe case of shingles. Halsey remarked *"The greatest sea battle of all time is about to take place and here I am taking baths in oatmeal."*

Nimitz came to Halsey inquiring who could take his place on the carrier USS Enterprise. Halsey recommended Rear Admiral Raymond Spruance.

In disbelief, Nimitz replied *"Hell, he's a Cruiser Commander"*.

Halsey backed up his choice stating, *"Yes, but he runs them fast enough to stay up with my carriers."*

Leading Allied naval forces to victory in the Guadalcanal Campaign, his ships remained at the leading edge of the Admiral Chester Nimitz's "island-hopping" campaign through 1943 and early

1944. In June 1944, Halsey was given command of the US Third Fleet. That September, his ships provided cover for the landings on Peleliu, before embarking on a series of damaging raids on Okinawa and Formosa. In late October, the Third Fleet was assigned to provide cover for the landings on Leyte and to support Vice Admiral Thomas Kinkaid's Seventh Fleet.

Resuming command in late-May, Halsey made a series of carrier attacks against the Japanese home islands. During this time, he again sailed through a typhoon, though no ships were lost. A court of inquiry recommended that he be reassigned, however Nimitz overruled the judgment and allowed Halsey to retain his post. Halsey's last attack came on August 13, 1945 and he was present aboard USS Missouri when the Japanese surrendered on September 2, 1945.

En route to Guadalcanal in a 4 engine US Navy flying boat, Admiral Halsey's pilot received a warning that a squadron of Japanese Zeros had just left the island. Halsey ordered the pilot to alter the course and head to Noumea, New Caledonia immediately. Admiral Halsey foiled the Japanese spies who obviously reported his departure from Pearl Harbor. They knew this type of aircraft would carry important personnel.

Fortunately, Admiral Halsey made it safely and immediately put his personal stamp on the operations. He seized headquarters, which Ghormley had never visited, ordered the officers to remove their ties and moved the fleet from Auckland to Noumea. Admiral Halsey strutted into our unit and every unit on the island.

When I met Admiral Halsey he lived up to the legend. In the brief period that he addressed our unit he instilled a confidence and courage in each of us. He personally reiterated his infamous slogan "*Hit hard, hit fast, hit often.*" Most importantly, he made us a promise that he was in the fight with us and he was.

As we assembled he personally assured each of us that we would no longer allow the enemy to call the shots. He vowed to take command and kill every son-of-a-bitch on this island and to be right there with us.

Admiral Halsey's arrival unquestionably bolstered our morale at a critical juncture. No one should underestimate the degree to which guides the outcome of any contest. Guadalcanal was no exception.

The six month campaign in Guadalcanal consisted of seven naval engagements, dozens of clashes and daily aerial combat.

Lockheed P38 Fighters

US intelligence learned of the Japanese Admiral Yamamoto's presence in Guadalcanal and discovered the details of his departure. As soon as his aircraft was airborne, our Marine Corp arrived with 8 Lockheed P-38 fighters and shot his plane down. I had the immense pleasure of witnessing this glorious moment flying some 6000 feet overhead when his plane hit the water. We knew he would never return to his flower gardens.

Following Pearl Harbor, the Navy's enlisted pilots became officers. My pilot, Lieutenant J.G. Murphy, stood among the greatest of pilots.

On October 16, 1942, while patrolling 200 miles Northeast of Espirito Santo we were jumped by a Japanese Zero Fighter. At the time, our aircraft patrolled the area from 4000 feet.

When the Zero initially appeared we descended to skim the water thus eliminating the Zero's ability to circle our aircraft and approach from all angles. His second approach came from the port side. Our port side waist gunner scored enough shots causing the Zero to emit smoke. But the Zero's shots took a toll on our port engine and we were also trailing smoke. On his third run at us, he shot across the wing section barely missing the fuel tanks. Ultimately his ammunition only made contact with the trailing edges of the wing, only 4 feet from my office in the coning tower. After that third attempt, the Zero gave up.

The attack left us 150 miles from Espirito Santo trailing oil from the left engine. Looking at the gauge, I reported that we had less than a gallon of oil remaining. Holes dotted the left side of the aircraft and the port engine.

Two days later, with the holes in the aircraft patched, a new oil tank installed, and other repairs made we were back on patrol.

In my experience, the reputation of the Japanese pilots as the best and the bravest is exaggerated. Although some of them may have been, I certainly encountered plenty who turned tail and ran when our waist hatch gunners would raise the canopy to expose a 50 caliber machine gun. The Japanese Kamikaze tactics were not employed during the early part of the conflict.

Another motivator in our fight was the Japanese reputation for cruelty. The Japanese military enjoyed brutality. They used every devise known to mankind as a means of torture. The Japanese cut off prisoner's fingers to retrieve a ring; fed them dead rats; tied prisoners prior to beating them; placed tourniquets around men's penises to cause their bladders to burst; and forced prisoners to drink their own urine or feces.

By January 1, 1943 U.S. forces completely controlled Guadalcanal. Our squadron had orders to return to Pearl Harbor but to leave the planes behind. Nothing about the voyage approached luxury. In order to gain passage on the U.S. freighter bound for Hawaii, we had to first unload the vessel. Once aboard, we had fresh drinking water but not a drop for any other use. I recommend neither shaving nor bathing with salt water. Fortunately, a rain storm during the voyage provided us with our only immersion in water the whole trip.

European Theatre

Our return to Pearl Harbor began a series of changing directives. Now we were to travel to San Diego, commission a new squadron of PB-Ys and return to the South Pacific. The heavy cruiser USS Detroit transported us to San Diego where our orders changed. Now, we began training in the first PB4Ys, the naval designation of a B-24 bomber.

Dunkeswell Devonshire, England

We formed squadron VB-103. After a month we transferred to Argentina, Newfoundland for two more months of training.

On April 1, 1943, the Navy transferred us to Dunkeswell Devonshire, England, approximately 100 miles from London. I was in the European Theater for 15 months patrolling the English Channel and the Bay of Biscay on the Western Coast of France. During patrol, enlisted crewmen were required to wear the Royal Air Force uniform with an American flag sewn unto the left shoulder. The Navy Enlisted Chambray shirt and jeans were not considered uniform. If captured, we would be executed as spies.

Our crew consisted of 11 men: the pilot, co-pilot, navigator, plane captain, bombardier, 2 radiomen, 2 waist gunners, a tail turret gunner and a tunnel hatch gunner. I acted as the plane captain and top turret gunner.

The PB4Y had no pressurization and therefore no heat. We wore electric heated suits that rarely worked and 10,000 feet above the English Channel was quite brisk. These early model PB4Ys had two 50 caliber machine guns in the nose, which could not be used effectively. They were free moving guns. The German fighter pilots recognized this and attacked the PB4Y head-on. We lost two aircraft due to this deficiency. Also, the fuel panel was located behind the bomb bay and up over the center section of the wing called the fuel transfer panel. As the plane Captain and top turret gunner, it was my responsibility to climb up to the wing during flight and physically change the hose connection to transfer fuel. The later model corrected both of these defects.

PB4Y-1 Official U.S. Navy Photograph, from the collections of the Naval Historical Center.

I lived in a round metal Quonset hut in Dunkswell along with the other members of my crew and another flight crew. During my one 7 day leave I visited London and experienced Buckingham Palace, Big Ben, the changing of the guard and even some night clubs. But my primary English experience consisted of patrolling the area.

Quonset Huts. Photo from Seebee Museum and Memorial Park.

Jack Holder's Squadron (Jack is kneeling, first row, left).

Christmas 1943, Dunkeswell Devonshire, England

While on patrol, we regularly encountered German Messer Schmidt 109's and Fokker III, German fighter aircraft. Upon discovery of one of these aircraft, we had the choice to fight or dive into the clouds for cover. Occasionally, the cloud protection strategy would fail and a German fighter would be waiting. I returned from some flights with perforated fuselage but never lost an engine or had a fellow crewman sustain an injury. I survived 56 flight missions over the channel and the bay.

I had the pleasure of shooting down one German Messerschmitt 109 Fighter. We had just emerged from cloud cover when the 109 crossed in front of us. Without even time to reposition the gun turret, I instinctively pressed the two triggers and watched as the 109 exploded. Relief, adrenaline and joy shot through my body.

German Messerschmitt 109 Fighter. From War History Online.

On one occasion, I received credit for a kill of a German submarine. Another PB4Y crew joined us in making two runs over a submarine as it surfaced. We each dropped two 1000 pound bombs. Diving on an enemy sub through a hail of anti-aircraft and machine gun fire it was something like Christmas and the Fourth of July, but it is far too early to begin the celebration. Celebration comes after you have returned to your home base, and in this case it was joyous affair.

I transferred to Chincoteague, Virginia in July 1944. I was awarded distinguish flying cross for meritorious service for antisubmarine patrol over the English Channel. I flew 56 missions over the English Channel and the Bay of Bisque.

Jack Receiving the Distinguish Flying Cross, 1946

The contents of the letter received from the Secretary of the Navy.

THE SECRETARY-OF THE NAVY
WASHINGTON

The President of the United States takes pleasure in presenting the
DISTINGUISHED FLYING CROSS TO
JOSEPH NORMAN HOLDER
AVIATION MACHINISTS MATE FIRST CLASS
UNITED STATES NAVY
for service set forth in the following:

CITATION:

For heroism and extraordinary achievement in aerial flight as an Air crewman of a United States Naval Patrol Bomber Plane in Anti-Submarine operations in the Day of Biscay and the Western Approaches to the United Kingdom from April 1, 1943 to June 25, 1944 .Completing his 56th mission during this period, HOLDER contributed materially to the success of his squadron. His courage and devotion to duty were in keeping with the highest traditions of the United States Naval Service.

For the President,

James Forrestal

Copy to; Secretary of the Navy
Public Relations Navy Dept.
Ref;Bdawds Serial 925 of 7 Dec 46
Send Medal

Transposed letter of Distinguished Flying Cross notification, December 7, 1946

My assignment was to assist in training a new PB4Y squadron. But the European conflict was winding down so the new squadron was not commissioned. I remained in Virginia for ten months as plane captain.

My next transfer took me to a PB4Y-2 squadron in Pensacola, Florida, where I continued to serve as plane Captain. This was the Navy's version of the B-24. The aircraft featured a single tail surface, larger and more powerful engines and increased speed.

Picture of Jack and other sailors from his squadron, 1944. Jack is 2nd on the right.

I had a 15 day leave of absence. I headed back to Texas to visit my parents.

After a few days, I headed into Dallas for some excitement. I asked the cab driver where I could find some action and he directed me to the Pirate's Cave. I met an attractive cocktail waitress.

Nothing much occurred that January, 1943, but when I transferred to England we began a regular correspondence.

In July 1944, the Navy sent me to Virginia and the minute I had a leave I went to Dallas. Things turned more serious and on my final transfer to Florida, Carleta and I were married November 6, 1945. It was not a very happy marriage. No children were involved. We stayed married and 2006 she developed Alzheimer's and I took care of her for 3 years until it got too much for me. In 2009 I placed her in a nursing home.

In October 1946 I transferred to a Naval R5D Transport Squadron in Patuxent River, Maryland. I was designated as a plane captain. The commercial realm referred to this aircraft as the Douglas DC-4 Aircraft. Several airlines flew the DC-4 in the 1940s and early 1950s.

Navy R5D Commercial DC4

After a turbulent 7 years, 10 months and 5 days, I honorably departed the service of the United States Navy. Aside from the vast experiences, I emerged with several accommodations and awards: 2 Distinguished Flying Crosses, 6 Air Medals, an American Defense Medal, an American Campaign Medal, a European African Middle Eastern Campaign Medal, an Asiatic Pacific WWII Campaign Medal, Presidential Unit Citation, Combat Action Commemorative, Combat Service Commemorative, Airborne and Assault Commemorative, Overseas Service Commemorative, Navy Commemorative, Honorable Service Commemorative, 2 Good Conduct Medals, 6 Meritorious Citations signed by the Secretary of the Navy and 1 Citation Signed by the President of the United States.

Post-WWII

The U.S. Navy awarded me an honorable discharge as an Aviation Machinist Mate First Class on March 5, 1948 in Washington D.C.

I moved immediately to Dallas, Texas. Braniff International Airways offered me a position as Apprentice Mechanic. Each year yielded a promotion. Within two years, I arose to Master Mechanic. Braniff afforded me the opportunity to obtain my Commercial Flight Engineer Certificate.

I moved to California for an aircraft mechanic position with Northrop Aircraft. I relocated 5 miles from the L.A. Airport to Hawthorne Airport. The job was tedious. After a couple of months, I peered across the runway and saw the insignia of my old company BRANIFF plastered across two DC-4 aircrafts. My curiosity piqued, I strolled across the runway and met Kirk Kerkorian, the owner of the aircrafts and of the Los Angeles Air Services (LAAS).

An Armenian multi-billionaire, Kerkorian developed a dusty desert town into the ritzy, glitzy Las Vegas. His legend originates from his development of famous Las Vegas hotels such as the Hilton and the original MGM Grand. He also owned the Metro-Goldwyn-Mayer film studio among other endeavors.

Three years my senior, the feisty billionaire still plays tennis at 96, and drives himself to his Las Vegas office in a Jeep. Although he became entangled in an infamous paternity suit, he was exonerated but he gave the child a 10 million dollar trust for when he reaches the age of 18. Kirk likes to keep a low profile. He has never allowed anything to be named after him, no matter how much money he has donated to a cause.

After the war, Kerkorian was a general aviation pilot and when he became wealthy, he bought Trans International Airlines, a charter service.

Kerkorian took a liking to me right off the bat and immediately hired me as a Flight Engineer. This meeting spurned years of a positive, professional relationship. I still have fond memories of watching Kirk walk around the casino floors followed by an attendant carrying a bag of silver dollars. Despite giving up high stakes gambling years before, he still liked to dabble in dollar slots.

Despite the fact that I had operated aircraft for years, the company grounded me in May 1952 when Kerkorian required that the Flight Engineers acquire pilot's licenses. Kerkorian wanted the engineer's to have the ability to double as the co-pilot. My previous flying experiences had not mandated a license.

Jacks Aircraft 1950: Luscombe-Silvaire

    I focused on getting back to the air and purchased a small disassembled aircraft, a Luscombe-Silvaire

    I rented an 18-wheel flatbed truck to transport the plane the 20 miles to the hangar at Hawthorne Airport. Restoring the dilapidated plane necessitated a general overhaul of the engine in addition to recovering the wing and other adjustments.

    My concentrated efforts returned the plane to airworthiness in record time enabling me to begin training in the aircraft during flight school. I arrived early to work where I acted as an aircraft mechanic in the interim. I flew before work, during my lunch break and again after work. By cramming in triple sessions daily, I had my Commercial Pilots Certification and an Instrument Rating within 6 months. I soloed on a Sunday morning and Kerkorian made a special trip to the airport to watch my flight. LAAS reinstated me as a co-pilot and Jack Holder was back in the air.

The LAAS schedule consisted of mainly chartered flights which varied the routes and times from one day to the next. One month my assignment could be a flight to Germany, the next to Japan. What my schedule lacked in consistency was made up for by the excitement.

I thrived in this atmosphere. I enjoyed shuttling soldiers from Japan to San Francisco, flying new automobile hardware from Detroit to Long Beach during a freight line strike and the thrill of undertaking a unique task each day. One assignment during the 1956 Hungarian Revolt entailed transporting Hungarian refugees from Munich to New York. These frightened refugees boarded the plane clutching a small loaf of bread and a few ounces of water. After much cajoling, the flight attendants finally convinced the refugees that they would be fed.

Suddenly, in March 1957 I received a call from Kerkorian's secretary informing me that my boss had sold all of LAAS's aircraft and the company was out of business.

Jack is Middle front, 1957, Union Oil DC3

Although disappointed, I would not be unemployed long. Union Oil Company of California ran an ad for an Aircraft Pilot. After an interview with the Chief Pilot and Vice President of the Aviation Department, I had a position as a co-pilot before the end of the month. Only a year later, my Airline Transport rating upgraded me to fly as the Captain.

My new company had 4 airplanes all based in Burbank, California. The small fleet was comprised of a Twin Beach C-52, a DC-3 and two Convairs. The flights traveled to multiple locations. Some frequently visited locales include Calvary, Platte River and Yellowknife Canada, as well as Newark, San Francisco, Lower California, La Paz, Jamaica, and Houston.

Union Oil Convair 580

I lived in various parts of L.A. from 1950-1960: Gardenia, Inglewood and eventually Westchester. Westchester bordered the L.A. International Airport and I frequented a spot called the Bar of Melody.

The Bar of Melody was only two miles from the airport and attracted plenty of airline personnel. It was a dark, dramatic venue that attracted intrigues and exploits. Its colorful owner, James

Marion, infamously plied his customers with free drinks before suggesting a whirlwind trip to Vegas.

James' epic gambling earned him a regular account in downtown Vegas. One fateful excursion, an alcohol soaked Jim was up $10,000 when his less intoxicated companion managed to drag him to the airport. Unfortunately, their flight back to LA was delayed and Jim finagled his way back to the Casino. By the time his friend got him on a flight back, Jim managed to squander his winnings plus another $15k.

Shortly afterward, Jim entered his bar to find two men in black suits at the bar. The ominous gentleman informed Jim in no uncertain terms that he had until 4pm the next day to shell out the $15 grand or hand over the deed to the Bar. Jim managed to save the bar and ultimately his marriage by ending the treks to Vegas.

My Bar of Melody brush with adventure began as I innocently enjoyed a cocktail at the bar. Ralph Waldron, an employee of Garrett Air Research Manufacturing Company, bellied up and sat next to me. Eventually, Ralph and I moved to a more secluded table in the restaurant. He revealed that he worked with the CIA.

"*We will deposit $10,000 in the bank of your choice. If you fly to Havana, drop leaflets. When you return, you will find another $10,000 in your account.*"

This trip was to be made in a Mitchell B-25 Bomber. I considered this for some time but my level headedness overcame my reckless side. I decided that the chances were pretty good that Castro would prevent my return flight from Cuba to Miami. I declined.

In early 1960, Pacific Aeromotive Company (PAC) converted the two Convairs from reciprocating engines to prop jets. The conversion altered them into machines that could fly 350 mph and had a range of 2900 miles.

On December 23, 1963, we had a scheduled trip from Houston, Texas to Midland Odessa, Texas. We were taking a Union Oil Vice President, Ray Burke, to his parents' home to spend Christmas. Much of Texas was under a severe weather storm. Ice covered the trees and the highways. The roads were practically impassable.

We approached Midland Odessa without incident. However, during the descent from 18,000 feet and upon reaching 7000 feet, we entered the overcast and encountered freezing temperatures again. On this leg of the trip the chief pilot was flying the aircraft and I acted as co-pilot. On the return trip to Burbank, California, the pilot and I would swap roles and I would act as pilot.

As the co-pilot my duties included de-icing the wing and tail sections. The job can be precarious as it entails removing ice from the aircraft's leading edge surfaces by applying heated air which is derived from the jet engine compressor at 360 degrees Fahrenheit. But, if the heat is left on too long it would warp the leading edge surfaces. I could see that no ice formed on the leading edge surfaces of the wings, but I could not see the tail.

The flight descent from 7000 to 2000 feet went smoothly. But when the approach flaps were made at 20 degrees the aircraft began to lose elevation control. During the final approach with 40 degree flaps applied the nose dropped. The aircraft nose gear hit the first light standard and sheared the gear.

The aircraft hit nose first and skidded down the runway 975 feet, engulfed in flames. I was knocked unconscious.

Jack's Accident December 1963

I came to and found myself still strapped in by the seat belt despite the seat's detachment from the floor of the plane. Unstrapping myself from the seat, I searched for a way out. Flames consumed the cabin. Desperate for an escape route, my only opportunity appeared to be the direct vision windows on either side of the cockpit. The windows measured a mere 10 x 12 inches as they only existed to enable the pilots to gain visibility in situations where the wind screen freezes over. I frantically tried to squeeze through the window but could not pull my hips through the small space. The airplane's only passenger, Ray Burke, managed to wrench my trapped body through the window to safety.

Meanwhile, the captain remained ensnared in the cockpit of the flaming aircraft. All efforts to save him failed. Finally, a Texas highway patrolman arrived after spotting the smoke from the plane. He grabbed an axe and rushed to the plane.

Desperately, he chopped a hole in the side of the cockpit and extracted the badly burned and still unconscious pilot. When the first fire fighters arrived on scene they discovered their truck had no chemicals necessary for extinguishing a fire.

Ray Burke and the cabin boy fractured their ribs and were treated and released. The captain spent 6 weeks hospitalized for severe burns. I fractured several vertebrae as well as sustained multiple cuts, bruises and burns. After three weeks, the Midland Hospital released me with a back brace I would have to wear for 6 months.

The National Transportation Safety Board determined that no pilot error contributed to the crash. However, this did not convince the Union Oil Vice President in charge of our aviation department. He hired an independent firm to further investigate the accident. The independent firm confirmed the lack of pilot error. Nonetheless, the company fired all personnel. The rationale being that any pilot having had a crash was more prone to have another.

Despite the unwarranted discharge, I remained undeterred. After a year of recuperating from the accident, I found a Pilot position with Lockheed Aircraft within a few months. Unfortunately, I never felt satisfied with this position. Friends from Allied Signal reached out to me about a position with them. I moved on after only four months with Lockheed.

My new endeavor took me back to Hawaii. My assignment entailed acting as the Engineering Service Representative to Hawaiian and Aloha Airlines.

I spent one year as a field representative with Hawaiian Airlines. I was transferred to Braniff Airways, Dallas, Texas. Spent four years there then transferred to London, England, BOAC and British European Airways. Spent five years there as supervisor of field service engineers.

April 1, 1975 transferred back to Phoenix, spent three years as customer service engineer with Allied Signal.

Texco Oil Company

For my next incarnation, I entered the oil business. Along with four partners, we formed "Texco" and I became its President and CEO.

My partners and I acquired oil leases in Texas, Oklahoma, Illinois and Louisiana. We drilled 26 wells in Oklahoma; 11 were dry holes but 15 emerged as producing wells. All 7 in Illinois were dry wells. Both the Louisiana wells were producers. In Texas two were producers and the third produced such a limited quantity we plugged the well.

The third Oklahoma well unexpectedly turned out to be a gas well. None of us had predicted either gas or oil at an upper depth level and did not take the precaution of implementing a blowout preventer. When we struck gas it became impossible to keep the drill bit in the hole. Gas began flowing through a seven inch diameter well bore casing creating tremendous pressure, 600 PSI.

For seven hours, the well spewed gas before a well control group could shut it off. The well covered a 360 degree area, some two miles in diameter. The police cordoned off the entire area and went door to door instructing people to shut off any flame producing devices.

The Oklahoma paper's headline read *"Small Independent Texas Oil Exploration Company Makes Large Gas Discovery in Okmulgee County, Oklahoma"*.

A company known as Texaco had filed cease and desist action for name infringement. Amid existing financial turmoil, I knew I had to act immediately. I instantaneously renamed Texco to "Onyx Petroleum".

During the late 1970s and until January 1983 investment money was easy to find. If the well was not productive the investor could write off the loss. However January 1, 1983 the tax structure changed. Any loss could not be written off and the investment money dried up.

My foray into the oil business would face additional strife. Ultimately, Onyx Petroleum never drilled a single well nor generated a nickel of revenue. Feeling foolish, I walked away from the oil business poorer yet wiser.

Allied Signal and Retirement

After only a phone call, Allied Signal decisively re-hired me as a mechanical engineer. I returned to Phoenix on April 1, 1984. The oil business behind me, I received a promotion to Engineering Manager and remained in that position until my retirement in December, 1991.

In 2010 my golfing buddies told me I needed to meet some lady to share my life and that I could not continue without a companion.

I went to a singles meeting and met a beautiful widowed lady, Ruth Calabro, who has become the treasure I wish I had met many years ago. I never really knew what love was until I met this wonderful person. At this writing we have been together for 4 years and 8 months sharing a beautiful life together.

Until I met this lady I never even told anyone I was a WWII veteran. She convinced me to become involved with other WWII veterans and tell my story. Since then I have given numerous presentations of my life including all my military life.

Navajo Code Talkers

July 2014 I was invited to the Intel Corporation to present and to hear a presentation by the Navajo Code Talkers.

The story of the Navajo Code Talkers began in 1940 when a small group of Chippewas and Oneidas became a part of the radio communications 32nd Infantry Division. The Sac and Fox tribes joined in the ranks as combat radiomen. The complexity of Navajo linguistics allowed it to become an ideal choice to be used in code due to the lack of documentation made available for learning to speak the language and ability for the same words to mean multiple things based on sound. (Navajo Code Talkers)

I enjoyed learning how the code was devised and enjoyed their performance.

Following their first dance I was asked to give a presentation.

Following my presentation the Code Talkers gave another dance and I was asked to join them.

Jack and Navajo Code Talkers Dance

One of our dancers threw two $1 bills on the floor and we danced around them. Upon completion of the dance one of the dancers picked them up and said *"Keep these for good luck."*

I now have them in a frame with a picture of the group.

Grand Marshal For Veterans Day Parade

Jack was nominated for the post by Brent Watkins a friend of Jack's from Real Estate School. "Jack is an inspiration to me and many others that you are never old to follow your dreams."

Veterans Day Parade, November, 2014. Jack and Ruth. Picture by Charles Gabrean.

This was a great honor for me and I will always remember the warm reception and the thousands of people that turned out for the parade to honor Veterans of all our Wars.

Pearl Harbor: 73rd Anniversary

Through the generosity of the Chives Charities and the Greatest Generation Organization I was among 12 WWII veterans returning to Pearl Harbor, December 2014.

The members attending were: George Norton, Thomas Petso, Michael M Ganitch, Clarence Byal, Robert Addobati, Samuel Clower, Robert Blum, Victor Miranda, John C. Seelie, Edward Stone, Lawrence Parry and myself.

Twelve Pearl Harbor Survivors Traveling to Pearl Harbor for the 73rd Anniversary. Jack is number 6 from the right.

Tuesday, December 2, 2014

I was aboard Hawaiian Airlines jet bound for Hawaii. This was a 7 night all expenses paid by The Greatest Generation Foundation and all of their sponsors.

We were treated like royalty. We stayed at the Hilton Hawaiian Village Waikiki Beach Resort. Just 3 miles from downtown Honolulu.

We were on the very tight schedule from 6:00 am until 9:00 pm. But what a glorious time.

Wednesday, December 3rd our first scheduled visit was the Hawaii Army Museum with Hawaiian school students.

National Memorial Cemetery of the Pacific

Second was a visit to the Punch Bowl National Cemetery. Dedicated to those men and women that served in the United Armed Forces. The walls of the memorial are etched with names of those who were never recovered from battle.

Our third visit was a welcome reception by the world famous Dukes in Waikiki, for a wonderful dinner.

Thursday, December 4, 2014

First stop was at Hickam Field air force base. This base was named after the Aviator Pioneer Lieutenant Colonel Horace Meek Hickam. Hickam is the Launch Point of Strategic Air Mobility and Operational Missions in support of the global war on terrorism.

Hickman Field Air Force Base

Second visit was to the Bowfin Memorial. The USS. Bowfin was a Baloa class submarine and was named after a voracious predatory fish native to the great lakes and Mississippi valley.

Bowfin Memorial

Next was the glorious private boat tour around Ford Island and a tour of the USS Arizona memorial, which is the resting place for the 1102 of the 1177 sailors killed on the Arizona during the attack on Pearl Harbor and Ford Island on December 7, 1941

USS Arizona Memorial

Friday, December 5, 2014

First stop was Schofield Barracks and Wheeler Army Base, School visit. Each of us were assigned to a different class room of young students. These children had prepared their classrooms with all types of greeting signs, etc. for the presenters. They were so appreciative.

Wheeler Army Base children's class room

Next was the Marine Corp Base Hawaii Ceremony with wounded warriors. This was at Kaneohe bay. This complete group of young marines were there recovering from some type of physical wound, but they were all in god spirits and so receptive.

Lastly was the Chive Charities meeting late afternoon. This reception was sponsored by the Chives Charities, President Mr. John Resig. The reception was held on the open grounds of the

Waikiki Hilton Hotel, with a crowd of more than 500 guests treated in proper fashion with food and drinks.

It so happened I was selected by our Greatest Generation Foundation President Mr. Timothy Davis to make the presentation for this crowd. This was such an honor and I did receive a momentous ovation.

December 6, 2014

This was a two hour session of signing autographs at the Hilton Hawaiian Hotel. From 10:00am to 12:00pm. Many people were still waiting in line when the ceremony was completed.

Signing Autographs at the Hilton Hawaiian Hotel. Jack is center right.

Next was a visit to the Missouri and the U.S.S. Oklahoma Memorial. The Oklahoma was sunk December 7, 1941 and never recovered.

USS Oklahoma Memorial

The U.S.S. Missouri is a United States Iowa class battle ship and was the fourth ship of the Navy to be named in honor of the U.S. State of Missouri.

Next was the visit to the battleship USS Utah Memorial. This was a sunset ceremony honoring those lost aboard the ship on December 7, 1941. It so happened this ceremony included the sea burial of a Utah Shipmate. His ashes were taken by two divers and placed inside the sunken Utah.

USS Utah Memorial

Sunday, December 7, 2014

First stop was Pearl Harbor visiting center. This was another long session of signing autographs to a very responsive crowd.

Next was commemoration brunch at Waikiki.

Next was a visit to the Oklahoma International commemoration. This memorial stands to honor the 429 sailors who lost their lives aboard the Oklahoma December 7, 1941. The Memorial stands on the shores of Ford Island next to the former berth of the Oklahoma. Those who escaped and swam ashore may have walked or crawled across this ground and to those sailors was a place of sanctuary and for us a place to remember.

Pacific Aviation Museum

This was the highlight of the trip. We visited the Pacific Aviation Museum and then to the VP-23 squadron hangar where I was 73 years ago. The building still standing untouched and with hundreds of bullet holes from the Japanese attack on December 7, 1941. VP-21 hangar 100 yards from ours was where the first bomb fell on Ford Island. It remains the same, heavily damaged. I walked down the aircraft ramp to the edge of the water where I spent 4 months in the beach crew. I then went to and spent time at the exact spot where I spent 3 days and nights in the sand bag constructed machine gun pit. Vivid memories ran rampant. I could still hear the ships and aircraft noise heard during blacked out nights.

Pearl Harbor International Parade

This was an occasion I will never forget. For the 12 of us riding as Grand Marshalls down the streets or Honolulu on the top of a new Corvette. We each had a new Corvette Convertible. The parade lasted one and a half hours and the crowd was estimated between 80,000 to 100,000 people.

We departed December 8, 2014 Honolulu back to Phoenix.

Publishers Remarks

When we are born there is nothing written, that we can see, about how our lives are going to be directed and the experiences we are going to have.

Each of us have our path. In a moment's notice it can change. The question is are we up to the task?

In working with Jack to write this book I feel honored to know him. He did indeed rise to the task.

From the farm boy in Texas to Pearl Harbor life was an adventure and the adrenaline, excitement and fear that Jack felt along the way lasted throughout WWII.

He never wavered in his belief in his country and he was surrounded by great men to lead the way to victory.